"Every soul needs a little strength training. In *Stronger Every Day*, Janell Rardon takes a comprehensive approach to address the things that weigh us down emotionally. The nine tools she shares effectively combine both scientific research and spiritual truths to provide the guidance needed to help the emotionally overwhelmed find a place of health and healing. This is an excellent resource for anyone battling emotional burnout or if you want to protect yourself from experiencing it in the future."

Saundra Dalton-Smith, MD, physician, speaker, and author
of *Sacred Rest: Recover Your Life, Renew
Your Energy, Restore Your Sanity*

"Janell Rardon's new book *Stronger Every Day* reads like a letter from a trusted friend. Her love and care shine through, along with an effective synthesis of the last fifty years of psychological and clinical wisdom, not to mention many eternal and biblical truths. She has structured this offering as a toolbox, gently introducing each new self-care tool with stories from her own life as well as quotes from many of the leading scholars and researchers of psychology and personal growth. The overriding message of the book is about gentleness—leading ourselves from the pit of shame, self-judgment, and limitation to the heaven of self-forgiveness, empowerment, and connection. Janell speaks with authority as one who has brought both herself and her clients through this journey, and now she passes on the keys to this process for all to use. Her Heartlift method puts biblical truth alongside a solid grounding in affective, cognitive, and behavioral neuroscience. One is left with the impression that timeless wisdom has been proven and brought to life with modern scientific research. I am very pleased to see her work reach a larger audience, and I am sure that she will uplift and inspire many people with this well-written and enjoyable book."

Benjamin Perkus, PhD, psychologist and creator
of the Aroma Freedom Technique

"Janell Rardon provides a pathway of transformation for people seeking to heal and grow by translating the key foundational aspects of a good psychotherapy process into practical tools and accessible language. She wisely puts a practical step-by-step method for addressing the heart and building emotional strength at the center of this process."

Beatrice Chestnut, author of *The Complete Enneagram: 27 Paths to Greater Self-Awareness* and *The 9 Types of Leadership: Mastering the Art of People in the 21st Century Workplace*

"Janell Rardon's book *Stronger Every Day* beautifully weaves Scripture, science, literature, and contemplative practices into a tapestry of tools to move us from a 'history of hurts' to a 'vision of victory.' Having worked in the field of child protection and family strengthening for nearly thirty years, I can't wait for our staff to read this book together to learn and grow stronger for the sake of the children and families we serve. Emotionally healthy adults serve others better. Janell spent time with us in Thailand a few years ago, speaking at a conference to women from over thirty nations. Her authenticity and biblical insights inspired and challenged us to be the best healthy self we could be. Her new book does that as well."

Kimberly Quinley, executive director, Step Ahead Foundation, Thailand

"Janell Rardon presents an in-depth look at a much-needed subject—healing from trauma. Social psychologists have highlighted the deep wounds that life sometimes brings. Rardon's book draws upon a broad and profound reservoir of spirituality to bring emotional health to a world in search of deep healing. Read this creative prose and enter into your own journey of strength for everyday life!"

Antipas L. Harris, PhD, president and dean of Jakes Divinity School and author of *Is Christianity the White Man's Religion? How the Bible Is Good News for People of Color*

"Janell's book *Stronger Every Day* is a powerful, detailed step-by-step process to healing the broken heart, leading one to wholeness and to a deeper, intimate relationship with Jesus. As always, Janell is passionate in her quest to see people healed and living the life Jesus died to give them."

Allison Rolston, PA-C, brain health coach

"In *Stronger Every Day*, Janell Rardon offers practical tools for emotional healing that are grounded in biblical principles and offer encouragement for the arduous journey toward wholeness. Rardon weaves her own journey of healing throughout the book, assuring you there is hope and freedom in your future. Whether you struggle daily with emotional wounds or only occasionally feel their presence, *Stronger Every Day* will equip you to move forward toward emotional health and wellness."

Kathy Howard, Bible study teacher and author of *Unshakeable Faith: 8 Traits for Rock-Solid Living*

STRONGER
Every Day

STRONGER
Every Day

9 TOOLS FOR AN
EMOTIONALLY HEALTHY YOU

JANELL RARDON

Revell

a division of Baker Publishing Group
Grand Rapids, Michigan

© 2021 by Janell Rardon

Published by Revell
a division of Baker Publishing Group
PO Box 6287, Grand Rapids, MI 49516-6287
www.revellbooks.com

Printed in the United States of America

Library of Congress Cataloging-in-Publication Data
Names: Rardon, Janell, 1959– author.
Title: Stronger every day : 9 tools for an emotionally healthy you / Janell Rardon.
Description: Grand Rapids, Michigan : Revell, a division of Baker Publishing
  Group, 2021.
Identifiers: LCCN 2020024618 | ISBN 9780800737580 (paperback)
Subjects: LCSH: Mental health—Religious aspects—Christianity. |
  Christianity—Psychology.
Classification: LCC BT732.4 .R37 2021 | DDC 248.4—dc23
LC record available at https://lccn.loc.gov/2020024618

ISBN 978-0-8007-4040-5 (casebound)

Some names and details have been changed to protect the privacy of the individuals involved.

This publication is intended to provide helpful and informative material on the subjects addressed. Readers should consult their personal health professionals before adopting any of the suggestions in this book or drawing inferences from it. The authors and publisher expressly disclaim responsibility for any adverse effects arising from the use or application of the information contained in this book.

21 22 23 24 25 26 27   7 6 5 4 3 2 1

Dedicated with deep gratitude to my three remarkable children,
Candace, Brooke, and Grant.

As Russian novelist Fyodor Dostoevsky once said,
"The soul is healed by being with children."
Each of you has healed my soul,
taught me the joy of living a wide-awake life,
and loved me unconditionally.
Because of you, I grow stronger every day.

Contents

Acknowledgments

William Arthur Ward once said, "Feeling gratitude and not expressing it is like wrapping a present and not giving it." This book is a gift and it is wrapped in the love, support, and strength of so many.

To Rob, the love of my life. This work is our work. Together, we journey toward emotional health and wholeness and as a result *grow stronger every day*. I truly believe "the latter . . . will be greater than the former" (Hag. 2:9 AMP), and I know that the best is yet to come.

To my big brother, Mike, and big sister, Susan. We have overcome hurtful words and learned the power of speaking healing words and as a result, I believe we *are growing stronger every day*. I finished this book at a critical time in our mother's life, and you gave me the support and space to put my heart and "our story" on paper. I think of the words of the great George Bernard Shaw, who once said, "If you cannot get rid of the family skeleton, you may as well make it dance." Here's to more years of dancing, laughter, and deep joy. I love you both.

To Mom. You kept the faith and fought the good fight. Your dying words to me were "Keep helping your ladies. They need to talk about their problems." Your final blessing fuels my mission. Thank you for allowing me to share "our story" of emotional healing. I love you.

To Aaron, Kristen, and Jose. You are answers to this mother's prayers. Thank you for loving my children and for making each of them stronger every day.

To my extraordinary editor, Vicki. In a hotel lobby, you took the time to listen to my heart. For that, I am most grateful. It is truly an honor to have this work of heart in your highly capable hands.

To my incredible team at Baker Publishing Group and Revell Books, what an honor to create this work together: Melanie Burkhardt, Janelle Wiesen, Mackenzie Gibor, Jean A. Entingh, Gayle Raymer, Eileen Hanson, Erin Bartels, and Gisele Mix. I am sure there are many I am missing. Each of you embody the words of Joseph Campbell: "A hero is someone who has given his or her life to something bigger than oneself." May you know you have great value, worth, and dignity.

To my clients, I say thank you. I'd love to name each one of you, but our work is kept in the vault of confidentiality. This book is a direct result of the hours and hours of our time together. On a daily basis, I am astonished by your commitment to transformation. Healing doesn't have to be complicated, and you are living proof of that.

To the Sage and Grace Essentials Community. You welcomed me, loved me, mentored me in Young Living essential oils, allowed me to practice Aroma Freedom Technique, and most importantly, shared a connection that is true koinonia.

To Teresa Hermann, my mentor and guide with Aroma Freedom Technique. Our weekend in Charlottesville was pivotal and literally transformed my life, both personally and professionally. What an honor to be your student.

To Dr. Benjamin Perkus, founder of Aroma Freedom International. Your emotional healing modality, Aroma Freedom Technique, has been a direct answer to prayer. Witnessing men, women, and children break free from childhood trauma has been highly rewarding.

To the Stronger Every Day community, thank you. You heartlift me and call me higher. We are so much better together, aren't we? Here's to sharing our message of hope and healing with the world.

Finally, to Jesus, for helping me find my way home. There were times I felt I wouldn't make it, but you stayed by my side, caught my tears, and remained faithful. Because of you, I am clothed with strength and dignity and smile at my future (Prov. 31:25).

The Heartlift Journey

2

Welcome God into
your space. Commit
to becoming stronger
every day.

1

Take the first step.
Begin living your
God-breathed life.

3

Find a therapist, certified
life coach, wise mentor,
accountability partner, or
like-minded small group
committed to emotional
health and wellness.

4

Take a look at
your history of hurts.
Begin making
peace with
your past.

6

Implement the tool
of memory
reconsolidation.

5

Begin crafting your
"Vision of Victory."

7

Breathe and believe
your new intentions
and affirmations.

Visit janellrardon.com

A Prayer for Strength

FROM MY HEART TO YOURS

You Are Stronger Every Day

Dear God,

Today is a brand-new day filled with endless possibilities.

Please come alongside my new friend.

May her heart and mind be healthy and whole.

May she lean in and know that she is not alone on this journey.

As she picks up her pen to start writing new words, new thoughts, and new vision,
assure her of your presence.

Help her as she begins using these brand-new emotional-health tools.

May she speak healing words into her future.

Affirm her value, worth, and dignity, every single day.

Allow her to feel, in her deepest core, a profound sense of security and strength,
and that she is getting stronger every day.

Remind her that when she is weak, you are strong.

May the unfolding of your Word give her the exact amount of light she needs for today.

May the peace that passes all understanding quiet every
worry.
May joy unspeakable and full of glory rise up in her soul.
May she find herself laughing out loud and recognizing
beauty like never before.
May things that once bothered her now cause less
agitation, anger, or frustration.
May ease and calm follow her throughout the hallways of
her home.
May resilience and rest enable her to respond with
remarkable grace.
When the new healthy narrative feels strange and even
uncomfortable—and it will—
empower her to continue using her new tools until her
new normal is
established.
When fear tries to overtake her newfound sense of calm,
send your powerful Spirit
to conquer its hold.
At the end of the day, when her head hits the pillow, may
she sleep in peace.
Most importantly, may she always remember she is
clothed with strength and dignity,
smiling at her future (Prov. 31:25).
Amen.

Introduction

WHERE THE LIGHT ENTERS

THE INTENTION:
I commit to becoming stronger every day.

The wound is the place where the Light enters you.

Rumi

One sunny May morning, I was lost in work when the doorbell rang.

I scurried from my upstairs office to find a big brown box on the front porch.

"Thank you!" I yelled to the UPS driver. "Have a great day."

With Mother's Day around the corner, I suspected it might be a gift from one of my three children. Having long ago identified gifts as my primary love language, I couldn't help but sit down and open it right there on the porch. As I ripped off the outer layer of sticky mailing tape and opened the box, I saw a package tucked under protective shipping peanuts.

Gently, I lifted it out and placed it before me.

Inside I found a medium-sized mint-green box with the words *Kintsukuroi Lamps, Handmade with Love* printed on the top in bold black letters. As I brushed my fingers over the elegant imprint, I sensed something special was about to unfold.

I held my breath and opened the box.

Nestled inside was a simple little brown-and-tan bowl—small enough to cup in my hands. As I turned the bowl round and round in my hands, I noticed large cracks filled with some form of lacquer or glue.

A short note explained that this was no ordinary bowl.

It was a Japanese Kintsugi lamp.

A Better Repair Method

The ancient Japanese tradition of Kintsugi dates to the fifteenth century. Japanese shogun Ashikaga Yoshimitsu "accidentally broke his favorite tea bowl and sent it to China for repairs. When it was returned to him, pieced together with ugly metal staples, he charged his Japanese craftsmen with finding a more aesthetic repair method."[1] What resulted was sheer magic.

Their ingenious repair process, known also as "golden rejoining," celebrates the brokenness of an object—embellishing the cracks with urushi lacquer and precious golden dust—with the grand intention to embrace the imperfections, not hide them.

I make no claim to be anything like those gifted Japanese craftsmen, but I can identify with the earnest shogun's desire for a *better repair method*. As a trauma-informed therapist specializing in family systems, a great deal of my work is with brokenness— broken families, broken relationships, but particularly, broken hearts, souls, and minds. Many of my clients have spent years in counseling and therapy, so by the time they make their way to me, they are extremely tired of the entire process.

They too are looking for a better repair method.

Where the Light Enters In

Ever since receiving my own Kintsugi lamp, I've made it a tradition to place a new tea light in the center of my little tan-and-brown bowl and take a quiet moment to pray before every client session. With great reverence, I ask God to fill the cracks of my client's heart with his light. Seeing the glow from every crack in my bowl is a holy reminder that beauty does indeed come from broken places. This simple, seemingly ordinary act empowers me to hold space—that is, focus on my clients and support them as they feel all their feelings and listen between the lines of their stories in order to hear the heartbeat of their struggle.

With sincere intention, I cup their tears in my hands and do my best to repair the cracks of their hearts with the healing lacquer of God's lavish love and the precious golden dust of hope. As with a treasured Kintsugi lamp, the cracks are where the light enters, making their hearts even more valuable as they now shine with increased empathy, an enlarged capacity to love well, more grace and less shame, and a deep, abiding sense of personal value, worth, and dignity.

Emotional and Spiritual Synergy*

I'm so grateful for my clients' stories, for their willingness to endure their healing journey, and mostly, for their trust. Each client has led me to seek better repair methods for healing the broken places of the heart, mind, and body. As a result, this methodology, the Heartlift Method*—a fusion of counseling, coaching, and spiritual direction—and the nine tools of *Stronger Every Day* have been curated with great intention, study, observation, and prayer. Separately, each tool stands on its own merit, but when combined, the tools create an emotional and spiritual synergy that accelerates the healing process and optimizes the outcomes.

After years of putting my finger on the pulse of my clients' issues, common themes arose among their struggles. These themes were often rooted in the formative years of early childhood experiences and most often found where unhealthy patterns reigned over healthy ones:

Angry parents created angry households that instilled insecurity and instability.

Perfectionistic mothers passed on unrealistic standards and expectations.

---

* Asterisks indicate first use of terms included in the glossary.

22

Passive-aggressive parents repressed and mishandled dealing with conflict.

Secretive family histories brought confusion, heartrifts,* and decades-long grievances.

Legalistic religious traditions and rules oppressed authenticity and freedom.

Culturally based pressures pushed "doing" more, not "being" more.

Silent witnesses to childhood trauma wreaked long-term havoc on little hearts.

I began to see my role in our therapeutic alliance as primarily a heartlifter*—an artisan of the heart—who wisely and carefully provides a nurturing presence and grace-filled space for hearts to heal. This transformed a typical fifty-minute session into several hours, which I now refer to as a "heartlift intensive." You see, getting to the core of the matter is not for the faint of heart. It takes time, energy, vulnerability, and tremendous courage.

The Journey from Our Heads *into* Our Hearts

Each of the three phases of the heartlifting journey—reflect, reframe, and re-author—invites us to enter into a transformational process that brings our history of hurts* into the present long enough to make meaning from and peace with our past so that we can move forward into our vision of victory* (future freedom).

This process requires moving *out* of the land of unhealthy and *into* the land of "all things healthy." Visualize it as the all-important journey from our head (head knowledge) *into* our souls (heart knowledge). How many times have you heard someone say,

"I know it here (pointing to their head), but I can't get it to go here (pointing to their heart)"? This forward movement helps us navigate from thinking to feeling—as painful as that might be.

Rewiring the neural pathways of our brains takes time. What took years to nestle into the folds of our brains won't suddenly disappear overnight. Yes, miracles happen; I never discount the power of God. But in my experience, change happens one changed thought process at a time. Very often, our skewed thought processes skew our perception of God and faith. Once we heal our mind, our perceptions—that is, our capacity for comprehension— heal, and we see more clearly. This doesn't come quickly, but it does come. In other words, we can't put it on our to-do list one morning and check it off later that night:

Stop belittling myself. Check.

Give up the grudge. Check.

Handle my anxiety better. Check.

Let go of my deeply rooted anger. Check.

Stop hating my coworker. Check.

Make peace with my father. Check.

Set mental and emotional boundaries.* Check.

Get over childhood trauma. Check.

If it were only that easy! But it isn't. If I had a magic wand, I'd swoosh it over you right now, but would that be the best thing? Transformation, from the inside out, invites us to participate. It asks us to take a risk, set aside valuable emotional energy, and find safe, healing communities where we can "unlearn" the unhealthy behavior patterns and communication skills we've developed over the years. Ultimately, it asks us to release our seeming control of things, which for most of us is inextricably painful. But as we say yes to this movement within—from head space into heart connection—we allow God the much-needed room to move freely. When our yes comes from a sincere willingness to become all God created us to be, I really believe God smiles.

Turning the Lights On

God responds to our yes by endowing and equipping us with every-thing we need to make the changes. Our brains can be rewired. Scientists call this neuroplasticity—the brain's God-given capac-ity to form new neural connections. Each one of our nine shiny new emotional-health tools is specifically designed to turn the lights on inside the limbic system* of our brain—the part of the brain "most heavily implicated in emotion and memory. . . . This system categorizes the experience of an emotion as a pleasant or unpleasant mental state. Based on categorization, neurochemicals such as dopamine, noradrenaline, and serotonin increase or de-crease, causing the brain's activity level to fluctuate and resulting in changes in body movement, gestures, and poses."[2] On your Stronger Every Day journey, you will get to know the limbic system very well. See the illustration that follows.[3]

- The amygdala, responsible for multiple emotional re-sponses, such as fear, love, sexual desire, and anger, is con-sidered the brain's watchdog[4]—housing our fight, flight, freeze, fawn[5] instinctive survival mechanism.
- The hippocampus interacts with the amygdala and creates memories with emotional ties. It also regulates motiva-tion, memory, emotions, and learning.

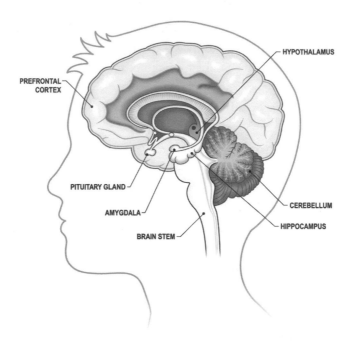

- The prefrontal cortex, located near the front of the head, involves decision making in response to our emotions. See this as command central as it controls empathy, insight, response flexibility, emotion regulation, body regulation, morality, intuition, attuned communication, and fear modulation.
- The hypothalamus feeds information to the amygdala and plays a role in the activation of the sympathetic nervous system, which is a part of any emotional reaction.[6]

Rewriting our stories—any and all of our unhealthy narratives*—and rewiring our neural pathways—living into a new, healthy narrative—won't happen without sheer grit (as we say here in the South) and good ole fashioned sweat and tears. The old, unhealthy behavioral patterns and communication skills have weaseled their way into deeply ingrained habits that don't want to change. The over one hundred billion neurons that make one hundred trillion neural connections inside our brains have gotten really comfortable traveling on those pathways.[7] Without our knowing it, many of these unhealthy thought and behavior patterns, absorbed from the emotional atmosphere of our early childhood, settle in and become "who we are." This happens on the subconscious level in our implicit memory,[8] which makes our task more challenging.

But today, you are making an incredibly brave choice.

This choice will have eternally profound ripples in your own life and in the life of your legacy.

I'm so proud of you, and I want you to know I am cheering you on.

Before the Journey Begins

Before we begin our Stronger Every Day journey, I'd like you to do something. After you finish reading this introduction, find a few moments and a quiet place, go to www.janellrardon.com, and listen to "Pick Up Your Pen," an audio meditative exercise that I recorded just for you. Imagine you're in your absolute favorite place in the entire world. It can be anywhere. The sky is the limit. Let the words of this story fill your heart with hope and peace.

I've included the meditation here, too, in case you don't have access to the internet. If you want to read it aloud, that is perfectly fine. Maybe you can ask a friend to join you and take turns reading it to each other. The most important part is that you read the words and let them soak deep into your soul.

Before you begin, take a deep breath and quiet your thoughts. Okay, ready?

Pick Up Your Pen

The alarm rings at 5:45 a.m. and welcomes a brand-new day. It rings at exactly the same time every day, except Saturday and Sunday, when it rings at 6:45 a.m. and graciously gives you an extra hour of sleep. As you roll over to the side of the bed, you notice something—two beautifully wrapped packages. They weren't there when you went to bed.

Curious, you pick them up. *What on earth are these?* you wonder.

After untying the bright blue ribbon on the first box, you open it and see a beautiful fountain pen inside. Also bright blue, like the sky. You pick it up and see three words etched in gold lettering: Stronger Every Day.

You repeat them: Stronger Every Day.

A little piece of paper reads,

> My flesh and my heart may fail,
> but God is the strength of my heart
> and my portion forever. (Ps. 73:26 NIV)

Even more curious to see what is in the next box, you place the pen down and untie the bright green ribbon on the second box.

Carefully, you fold back a layer of shiny white tissue paper to find a stunning leather journal etched with the same three words in gold lettering: Stronger Every Day.

As you take the journal out of the box, little golden stars of confetti fall around the journal like a golden halo.

Tears well up in your eyes, and your heart seems to smile. Just saying those three words out loud, Stronger Every Day, feels good.

Very, very good.

Overwhelmed, you place the pen on top of the journal, fold your hands, bow your head, and pray.

God, thank you.

I am so grateful that you are a God who gives fresh starts, new beginnings, and second chances.

I am so grateful that you are a God who breathes life into seemingly dead places.

I am so grateful that you are a God who sees, loves, and walks with me.

I am so grateful that you never give up on me, no matter what. When I fall, you pick me up.

I am so grateful for your lavish, unlimited grace. I want to understand it better.

I know a meaningful life is not free from pain or suffering but is one filled with the power and strength to overcome.

I know a meaningful life is not free from resistance or negativity but is one in which we stay with and pray through the pain.

I know a meaningful life is not free from hard times, loss, or grief but is one empowered by the Spirit.

God, today I begin living into a new story—a brand-new, God-breathed healthy narrative based on truth and love and grace.

Together, we will fill each page of my new journal with great truth and bright light—just like you promised me so long ago.

I want to become stronger every single day.

Above all else, help me embrace the healing words of this journey so that I can live the meaningful life you have planned for me. Amen.

In this book, the chapters will be referred to as "tools," and at the end of each tool, you will be invited to "Strength Training for the Soul," where together we will envision, educate, and establish ourselves to do the following:

- Gain understanding of the nine emotional-health tools in your shiny new toolbox.
- Experience the power of life-giving portions of Scripture through the ancient practice of *lectio divina*, contemplative prayer, and meditative exercises.
- Begin practicing another ancient tradition, St. Ignatius's daily examen, and increase self-awareness, implement a daily connection to God and self, and deepen your faith journey.
- Set intentions and craft affirmations for overcoming obstacles and initiating new belief systems.
- Activate memory reconsolidation* by "breathing and believing."[9]
- Rest, recover, and collect strength by adding life-giving practices into our daily routine. When we move through life from a place of collected strength, our hearts have more to give.
- Write—and here's where the fun begins. We get highly intentional about what we envision for our future and about implementing the threefold cord of emotional health and wellness: healthy sense of self, healthy behavior patterns, and healthy communication skills. This cord is our emotional-health legacy (Eccles. 4:12).
- PS: Don't be afraid of the writing part. As a former writing teacher, I promise it will be both fun and freeing. I've witnessed firsthand that the most reluctant of students fall deeply in love with the creative process of putting words on paper.

Let's get started.

Strength Training for the Soul

Today's Heartlift*: "Of all sad words of tongue or pen, the saddest are these, 'It might have been.'"

John Greenleaf Whittier[10]

Envision: A Time to Think

For years, I taught a middle and high school literature-based writing class. One of our favorite aspects of study was metaphors, especially those centered around the heart. Author Julie Beck writes about enduring literary metaphors of the heart:

> The English language is full of metaphors invoking the heart. People wear their hearts on their sleeves; they have hearts of stone or hearts of gold; they have heart-to-heart conversations. So, in the late 18th and 19th century, the peak of the process by which the heart was becoming objectified, you've got the rise of the Romantic poets who reinforced the idea that there was something very heartfelt about what lurks in our chest. Those languages of emotions being heartfelt, hearts rising and sinking, being heavy-hearted, light-hearted, having the heart of a lion and so on—those metaphors and the language in which we talk about the heart, show that we still, even at the very peak of scientific medicine, have those associations of the heart being psychologically and emotionally, even spiritually important.[11]

Your heart matters. It has value, worth, and dignity. In *Stronger Every Day*, you are going to experience real growth in the area of heart intelligence. Rollin McCraty affirms that "the most effective way to really reduce stress and anxiety and even feelings of overwhelm is to learn how to access the intelligence of the heart

31

and shift the rhythms of the heart, which sends a different neuro-message to the brain."[12]

Before we go any further, I invite you to sit at a table, either alone or with friends, or host a special night for your small group, and create a vision-of-victory heart board. Some life coaches and counselors use dream boards. Some use vision boards. I like to use a heart board. That's right, a simple heart. Proverbs 4:23 is at the core of our work: "Above all else, guard your heart, for everything you do flows from it" (NIV). So it seems fitting to use a heart-themed board. Be creative here. Use any type of board: foam board, poster board, wood, canvas, paper, and so on. This is *your* heart we are talking about. Use watercolors, magazine clippings, chalk, paint, mosaic tiles, jewels, seashells, rocks, and whatever else you would like. Create a heart in the center of the board or create a heart string (see the following illustration[13]). I suggest center placement because the heart is the center of everything in our lives. For more detailed information and creative ideas, visit www.janellrardon.com/resources.

As you begin your Stronger Every Day journey, take some time to do the following:

- Try to envision what you want your meaningful new story to be about. Old narratives, labels, and hurtful words don't have a space in your heart anymore. There is no room at the inn. It is time to write new narratives. Most importantly, there is no room for "it might have been" because we are pursuing meaningfulness and joy.

- Give some intentional thought to the "hows" and "whats" of your new narrative. Ask simple, thoughtful questions, such as "What does a healthy relationship look like?" or "Do I need to learn more about setting emotional boundaries?" This heartlifting work invites us to keep the threefold cord of emotional health and wellness in mind: healthy sense of self, healthy behavior patterns, and healthy communication skills. When we are healthy in these areas of our lives, everyone in our spheres of influence benefits. Consider these intentions (be as specific as you desire):

  - Heal a fractured friendship with _____

    _____.

  - Spend less time on social media, especially _____

    _____.

  - Learn to manage my anger. Yelling causes _____

    _____.

  - Give time and space to a close relationship that needs emotional healing.

  - Really listen to the person talking to me. I hear my friend saying, _____

    _____.

  - Volunteer for a nonprofit and expand my capacity to serve others.

Educate: A Time to Learn

Retention is one of the seven laws of the learner. You are learning an entirely new emotional-health language, the language of love, to help you live the life God designed just for you. Learning means reviewing repeatedly. Begin by taking a few moments to review the Heartlift Journey Chart and the glossary at the back of the book to familiarize yourself with the new heartlifting language. Refer to both as needed as you continue your journey.

Establish: A Time to Build

One of my favorite spiritual practices comes from St. Ignatius, a fifteenth-century Spanish Basque priest and theologian. At the center of his teachings is the daily examen,[14] a method to review your day and examine/set intentions for the next. Set aside fifteen to twenty minutes, sometimes less as this becomes more of an attitude or mental process than an actual practice. I've done it while standing in line at the grocery store. Many different interpretations have been written, but I use the following.

Below, I've added personal examples to help you:

1. Become aware of God's presence. In the Heartlift Method, I've adapted this to "Welcome God into your whys" or into the present moment. *God, I welcome you into the whys of my mother's medical crisis. I welcome you into this moment. Help me to be right here, right now.*

2. Review the day with gratitude. *God, by your grace, I faced another emergency room visit with my mom. As I focused on being present, I was able to regulate my emotions. Thank you for sending two chaplains whose presence really helped.*

34

Above all else, guard your heart (Proverbs 4:23).

A DAILY PRACTICE

Reflections based on the spiritual practice, The Examen, taken from
St. Ignatius of Loyola, a 15th century Spanish priest.

(1) BECOME AWARE OF GOD'S PRESENCE.

In the Heartlift Method, I've adapted this to "Welcome God into your whys" or into the present moment. Take a few deep belly breaths to inhale God's love and exhale any stressors or anxiety from the day's activities.

(2) REVIEW THE DAY WITH GRATITUDE.

As you reflect back on the day, make a mental list, or write in your heart journal, what you noticed as you moved through the day. Kind people? Beautiful scenes? A difficult, traffic-filled trip to work? A friend's call? A stranger's help?

(3) PAY ATTENTION TO SHORTCOMINGS.

Notice those moments where you perhaps fell back into old, unhealthy behaviors or patterns. Offer yourself grace, not shame. Ask God to help you in that area. Know that God's mercies are new every single morning and that you are getting stronger every day.

(4) CHOOSE ONE FEATURE OF THE DAY AND PRAY ABOUT IT.

Do you need to rewind and reset a situation? How can you reframe it and do better tomorrow? Do you need to ask for help in overcoming angry outbursts?

(5) LOOK TOWARD THE DAY TO COME.

A simple prayer to end the day: "Because of your great love I am not consumed, God, for your compassions toward me never fail. They are new every morning; great is your faithfulness toward me, God (Lamentations 3:22–23, NIV). Thank you for today. Amen."

Stronger
EVERY DAY
janellrardon.com

3. Pay attention to shortcomings. *I was impatient again, God, so I will collect strength in order to store patience in my weary soul. I lost my cool for a few minutes, but I went and sat in the hospital chapel and prayed for peace.*

4. Choose one feature of the day and pray about it. *Healing comes in various ways, God. Send nurses, doctors, or hospital workers to help my mother—and me—through this arduous journey.*

5. Look toward the day to come. *Tomorrow, I will wake up and go for a walk. This helps clear my mind for the day. I close the day now with the examen and pray for good sleep.*

PART ONE

Envision

ENVISION (v): To imagine as a future possibility; visualize; to picture mentally.

"For I know the plans I have for you," says the Eternal, "plans for peace, not evil, to give you a future and a hope—never forget that."

Jeremiah 29:11

TOOL 1

Step across the Threshold
MEANINGFULNESS

THE INTENTION OF TOOL 1:
I step across the threshold of my meaningful new story.

He had the vague sense of standing on a threshold, the crossing of which would change everything.

Kate Morton, *The Forgotten Garden*

Early one morning, when my thoughts wouldn't let me sleep, I flipped on the television to the HGTV channel. One of my favorite shows, *Fixer Upper*, with popular hosts Chip and Joanna Gaines, happened to be on. My favorite part of the show is watching this cute couple walk through the projected fixer-upper. Room by room, sometimes foot by foot and inch by inch, they gaze at every corner of the space—noting big and little changes they want to make:

Take this wall down.

Replace the old paneling.

Put new windows here.

Add space to the living area.

Give this outdated bathroom some shiny new tile.

Their visionary spirit and construction expertise see what the normal, untrained eye can't see. They always have a *better repair method* up their sleeves. This particular episode, I tuned in just as Chip feverishly, and with seeming great joy, demolished the siding of an old Texas farmhouse. Within minutes, only a solid lumber skeleton remained, known in the construction industry as "good bones."

Suddenly, Joanna ambled into the room and beamed that radiant smile of hers, the design wheels whirling in her head. She stepped across the threshold with a spring in her step.

"Ready for a new story?" she asked with gusto, lovingly brushing her hand against an antiquated wall as if talking to the house.

"Yep, it is time for this old farmhouse to have a new story, Chip. Let's do this."

Gutting to Good "Emotional" Bones

A few months later, while in Kansas to celebrate Thanksgiving with my son and his wife, I had a Joanna Gaines moment—lovingly brushing my hand against an antiquated wall—the rough, paint-chipped wall of my son's new, yet very old, recently purchased circa 1915 fixer-upper. When I stepped across the threshold, my heart sank. To the naked eye, this house looked like a lost cause. I thought, *Oh my, what has my son gotten himself into here? What must his bride of one year be thinking about all this?*

I wanted to call in an HGTV intervention and make it all better. Isn't that what good moms do? Make life easier? Save their children from any and all pain?

A wave of wisdom came over me. I stepped back to take it all in. Even if I could have given them a check for a million dollars (which I'm sure they would have gladly received), that would have gotten in the way and denied Grant and Kristen the incredible rewards of transforming this broken house into their home. This labor of love had to be done on their own.

My son shared his vision for their future family dwelling. As we walked around, peering in rooms, I watched his six-foot-five frame duck under eaves. Slowly and with great admiration, I caught his vision. He talked about his ideas for the master bedroom, the upstairs bathroom, and most importantly, the kitchen. Suddenly, he was ten years old again, sprawled out on his bedroom floor, surrounded by a million plastic building blocks, building a city or a park or an entire community. But this time, his creation was going to be real. With great pride, he shared his ideas:

41

Frame a closet here.

Add a window here.

Take out this wall.

Update the upstairs bathroom.

Rip up the carpet and let the solid wood floors shine.

Within minutes, I started seeing their home *through his eyes*.

I had often believed that all the hours he and his sisters spent building and dreaming with toy blocks would one day have real-life benefits. Thankfully, they did. I reassured myself that he would eventually figure out this bigger "design puzzle," and suddenly, I felt quite peaceful inside.

Before purchasing the house, they had learned it was a happy place. The original owners taught piano lessons, and the home was a hub in the neighborhood. To my son, this old house had simply lost its heartbeat. All it needed was someone to see it had good bones and to give it a chance. The heart of this fixer-upper had obviously called out and invited Grant and Kristen to do just that. Their inspiring vision took me out of my head (and its worry thoughts) and into my heart (and its faith thoughts).

As we meandered into the backyard, I sat down on an old, dilapidated bench left by the previous owners. History seemed to embrace me. I mentally picked up my pen and began writing a note to my future self.

Dear Future Self, Take this all in. Look at your grandchildren running and playing. Giggles and backyard adventures fill the air. Rounds of flashlight tag in the long days of summer. Snowball fights and snowman building in the harsh Kansas winters. Long talks about life and love and family.

I smiled inside and outside.

Kristen came and sat next to me. We played a game of catch with Midas, their golden Labrador retriever and my first grandpup. Between every exchange of the saliva-saturated bright green tennis ball, my lovely daughter-in-law and I shared a few meaningful moments together. Sitting there was an answered prayer and a dream come true. When my husband, Rob, and I were first dating, we talked for hours about our hopes and desires for the future, *a future that seemed a long, long way away.* Having come from unhealthy, alcoholic homes, we knew we wanted a committed relationship and a strong core of faith at our family center, and we desperately hoped for a God-sized legacy filled with a whole lot of healthy relationships, laughter, and love.

One truth had led us to this moment in time. "Many waters cannot quench love," writes wise King Solomon, "rivers cannot sweep it away. If one were to give all the wealth of one's house for love, it would be utterly scorned" (Song 8:7 NIV).

"There's something special about this place," I said to Kristen, smiling. Expectancy and joy filled the few crevices of worry that lingered in this mama's heart.

This house has good bones, I thought. *Really good bones.* It needs a great deal of work, yes, but what it really needs is a whole lot of love—the kind of love that money can't buy.

"I believe you and Grant are going to love this place back to life," I said. "It hasn't finished telling its story. It has a lot more to say."

Do You Need to Be Loved Back to Life?

I'd like you to think of *this book* as your emotional health and wellness fixer-upper. We'll walk through your heart, chamber by chamber, maybe heartbeat by heartbeat, in order to create a remarkable new heart—filled with everything it needs to live into a beautiful new story. Antiquated patterns of behaving and paint-chipped communicating skills will be made brand-new. We're gutting to your emotional bones, and the result is going to be glorious:

Take down this wall of defensiveness.

Replace an old grudge with forgiveness.

Rewire old triggers* lodged in your neural pathways.

Open new windows of joy, laughter, and freedom.

Add on an expansion of healthy emotional space.

You see, you have good bones. *Very good bones.*

You haven't finished telling your story, and I believe you have a whole lot left to say.

At the end of this journey, you will have a shiny, brand-new tool kit, filled with nine highly efficient and effective emotional-health-and-wellness tools designed to help you live into your healthy new story—filled with life, light, and a whole lot of love. We'll look for answers, and if we can't find the answers, we will keep asking, seeking, and knocking until we do (Matt. 7:7). When the renovation gets too hard or fatigue sets in, we will encourage one another. That's what we do.

First Things First

Kitchen and bath design and construction is our family business. Over the past thirty-some years, I've watched my husband gut thousands of homes. Watching this process never gets old. I've witnessed that same pensive, oft-intense, vision-filled look on his face. He sees what the normal, untrained eye can't see. It seems reviving the good bones of a house has been passed down from father to son.

Rob and Grant worked from sunrise to sunset gutting the kitchen and preparing it for electrical work, plumbing, lighting, flooring, insulation, and drywall. They moved walls, installed a brand-new picture window (right over the sink, of course, for viewing the front yard), and gave the entire space the new life it had been waiting for. Since the kitchen is the heart of the home, it seemed the perfect place to begin. Seeing Rob and Grant, father and son, do this together, was a bonus. Full-circle moments like these make life worth living and seem to bring, as my beautiful Kenyan friends say, "big joy, big laughter, and big gratitude." The words of poet Maya Angelou echoed: "I sustain myself with the love of family."[1] At the end of life, is there truly anything more valuable?

"You're going to have a strong heart," I said to the house while sweeping up the day's sawdust. "A really strong heart. I can't wait to celebrate holidays, birthdays, and so much more!"

In an odd way, the work my husband and I do is very similar. Rob works with kitchens (home renovation); I work with hearts (emotional transformation). He's taught me a great deal about the process of home renovation—and his lessons always seem to make their way into transformative life lessons. I think you'll hear hints and helpful tips as you listen between the lines of Rob's wise words:

- *Never be in a hurry.* Renovation requires patience. As the proverb says, "It is better to be a patient man than a mighty warrior, better to be someone who controls his temper than someone who conquers a city" (Prov. 16:32).

- *Remember that nothing of great value is done quickly.* It takes time. Real life isn't as efficient as a one-hour HGTV show. Renovating and remodeling rarely go smoothly.

- *Expect the unexpected.* Things will go wrong. Sounds pessimistic, but sadly, it is true. Ask any subcontractor. They'll tell you this maxim is solid. I'm 100 percent certain that is why Moses told his protégé, Joshua, "Be strong and courageous. Do not be afraid; do not be discouraged, for the LORD your God will be with you wherever you go" (Josh. 1:9 NIV). Transformation requires courage. It asks us to stay with and pray through the process.

- *Have a well thought out plan.* Design demands accurate measuring. Jeremiah 29:11–12 assures, "'For I know the plans I have for you,' says the Eternal, 'plans for peace, not evil, to give you a future and a hope—never forget that. At that time, you will call out for Me, and I will hear.'" Rob's customers call frequently, and now, text or email often. As we call on God, he will unfold his plan and design. We just have to listen.

- *Rent a dumpster or big truck.* Haul away the trash—the old, worn-out, not-working-anymore stuff. Have plenty of trash bags and cleaning supplies on hand. It gets really dirty, really fast. To haul something is to pull or drag with effort, initiative, or force. I love the prophet Isaiah's words: "They will rebuild ancient ruins and restore the places long devastated; they will renew the ruined cities that have been devastated for generations" (Isa. 61:4 NIV). It will get really dirty, really fast when it comes to changing how you think. Our old ways of thinking and behaving won't go away without effort, initiative, and sometimes force. With as much strength as it takes to haul away the trash physically, we must haul away the old, worn-out, not-working-anymore thought processes. They are rutted and ridged within the folds of our brains and very, very comfortable. But we are stronger than they are, and it is time for them to go.

- *Prepare the room.* Gut to the good bones. The psalmist David gives us the first step necessary for our heart renovation. "Create in me a clean heart," he prays to God. "Restore within me a sense of being brand new" (Ps. 51:10). I love this version's interpretation of David's plea: create hints at making something out of nothing. It assures us that we can live into our beautiful new story.

- *Tear down any and all walls that need to come down.* Out with the old, in with the new. Eugene Peterson helps us understand the labor and effort involved in writing a new narrative. He interprets the apostle Paul's words this way: "We use our powerful God-tools for smashing warped philosophies, tearing down barriers erected against the truth of God, fitting every loose thought and emotion and impulse into the structure of life shaped by Christ. Our tools are ready at hand for clearing the ground of every obstruction and building lives of obedience into maturity" (2 Cor. 10:5–6 MSG). New narratives are not only possible, they are promised.

- *Acquire new tools and equipment.* New beginnings mean new equipment—new ways of seeing and doing things. With every new appliance comes an owner's manual. With every new year, technical advancements test the learning curve. My husband is always being challenged by new ways of doing things. Once again, Paul shows us the way.

"Regarding your previous way of life," he instructs, "you put off your old self [completely discard your former nature], which is being corrupted through deceitful desires, and be continually renewed in the spirit of your mind [having a fresh, untarnished mental and spiritual attitude], and put on the new self [the regenerated and renewed nature], created in God's image" (Eph. 4:22–24 AMP).

• *Finally, celebrate!* Enjoy your beautiful new space. Isaiah invites us to "remember not the former things, nor consider the things of old" (Isa. 43:18 ESV). Invite friends and family over and let them see what God has done. Let them enjoy your brand-new emotional-health tools! They will revel in the joy of your new story.

Eudaimonia, the Pursuit of Meaningfulness

While Rob and Grant worked, Kristen and I took long walks—with Midas, of course, leading the way. I'm not proud of the fact that I didn't do a lot of the work, but my work involves mental labor, not manual labor. My time will come. I did help organize the makeshift kitchen and worked hard pulling up floor tile, but mainly we had girl time.

Their little town is delightful. East Coast meets Midwest—or the Great Plains, as I've been kindly corrected. College soccer led Grant to Kansas, and then God provided an entire life and a beautiful wife for him there. It's a slower life. Less traffic. Quieter ways of doing things. And a Main Street that could be the shining star of a Hallmark Christmas movie.

Grant chose to pursue a meaningful life—one of the tenets of human flourishing.[2] His choice didn't come easily, as moving far from home never does. We watched him struggle to find his way, to figure things out, and to consider what he wanted his life to look like. This involved hard-fought choices and decisions about career paths and relationships. In the end, the arduous journey made him a better man.

In "Pursue Meaning instead of Happiness," authors Emily Esfahani Smith and Jennifer Aaker help us understand the concept of *eudaimonia*:

> The distinction between happiness and meaningfulness has a long history in philosophy, which for thousands of years has recognized two forms of wellness—*hedonia*, or the ancient Greek word for what behavioral scientists call happiness, and *eudaimonia*, or what they call meaningfulness. The happy life is defined by seeking pleasure and enjoyment, whereas the meaningful life is bigger . . . connecting and contributing to something beyond the self, which could be your family, your work, nature, or God. . . .
>
> The meaningful life is often characterized by stress, effort, and struggle. . . .
>
> When people say their lives are meaningful, . . . it's because they feel their lives have purpose, coherence, and worth.[3]

The concept of *eudaimonia* hails from the work of ancient philosopher and scientist Aristotle (384–322 BC) in his studies and writings on the science of happiness. Brent Strawn writes, "The philosophical study of happiness is as old as Aristotle and, in truth, is older than him. But Aristotle is seminal, and his work on what constitutes the good life is a starting point for many serious discussions of happiness today. This holds true for the most recent extensive and empirical study of happiness, which is the purview of Positive Psychology."[4] The pursuit of *eudaimonia*, or meaningfulness, most often involves stress, effort, and struggle and doesn't cultivate immediate happiness. But it does ultimately make us better people.

When I frame this concept biblically, I lean toward the powerful prayer of the apostle Paul to the church in Ephesus:

> For this reason, I kneel before the Father, from whom every family in heaven and on earth derives its name. I pray that out of his glorious riches he may strengthen you with power through his Spirit in your inner being, so that Christ may dwell in your hearts through faith. And I pray that you, being rooted and established in love, may have power, together with all the Lord's holy people, to grasp how wide and long and high and deep is the love of Christ, and to know this love that surpasses knowledge—that you may be filled to the measure of all the fullness of God. (Eph. 3:14–19 NIV).
>
> Now to the God who can do so many awe-inspiring things, immeasurable things, things greater than we ever could ask or imagine through the power at work in us, to Him be all glory in the church and in Jesus the Anointed from this generation to the next, forever and ever. Amen. (vv. 20–21)

This prayer is my prayer for you. In reading this book, I pray that you will be filled to the measure of the fullness of God. When you face stress, effort, and struggle, may you remember Paul's words and be strengthened. That is true *eudaimonia*, and I want it for you.

In order to accomplish this, you will need new tools—nine to be exact—chosen carefully, just for you. Let's look at the three compartments in your shiny, new tool kit:

1. *The Envision Tools (meaningfulness, secure attachment,* and cognitive reframing*).* The envision tools invite us to imagine and visualize future possibilities. An ancient

proverb tells us, "As [a man] thinketh in his heart, so is he" (Prov. 23:7 KJV). This vital truth guides our time in this compartment as we restore a strong, secure sense of self, reframe our thought processes, and develop our understanding of what *eudaimonia*, the pursuit of meaningfulness, looks like on a daily basis.

2. *The Educate Tools (self-compassion, healthy assertiveness, and spiritual growth).* The educate tools equip us with wisdom, knowledge, and instruction. In a sense, we are going back to our God-created beginning (Gen. 2:7)[5] to relearn the truth about ourselves. Wise King Solomon's words will guide our time in this compartment: "Good friend, don't forget all I've taught you; take to heart my commands. They'll help you live a long, long time, a long life lived full and well. Don't lose your grip on Love and Loyalty. Tie them around your neck; carve their initials on your heart. Earn a reputation for living well in God's eyes and the eyes of the people. Trust GOD from the bottom of your heart; don't try to figure out everything on your own. Listen for GOD's voice in everything you do, everywhere you go" (Prov. 3:1–6 MSG). This vital truth guides our time in this compartment as we focus on the power of self-care, find healthy ways of using our voices, and spend time in spiritual formation.

3. *The Establish Tools (memory reconsolidation, emotion regulation, and human connection).* The establish tools enable us to live in newfound authority—based on God's redemptive power working in and through our lives. This was Jesus's legacy. His last words on earth established his disciples and enabled them *from that moment onward* to do great things. He spoke this unction loud and clear:

"The person who trusts me will not only do what I'm doing but even greater things, because I, on my way to the Father, am giving you the same work to do that I've been doing. You can count on it. From now on, whatever you request along the lines of who I am and what I am doing, I'll do it. That's how the Father will be seen for who he is in the Son. I mean it. Whatever you request in this way, I'll do" (John 14:12–14 MSG). This vital truth guides our time in this compartment as we consolidate negatively charged memories, practice emotion regulation, and open our hearts to deeper joy and connection with others.

4. And, in a hidden compartment inside the box are your most important tools—your brand-new pen and heart-lifter journal—because you are a heartlifter-in-training. Somewhere in life, you either put your pen down (as I did) or someone took it from you and started writing their version of your life story. Today is an extraordinary opportunity to take your first big step of faith across the threshold of your future. As you pick up your pen and start writing your meaningful new story, all of heaven will be cheering you on. Can you see a host of angels jumping up and down right now? *Yes! She's picking up her pen again! Go for it! Woo-hoo!* (Okay, I added the "Woo-hoo," because that is my mojo, but I know there is a lot of excitement in the heavenlies over your new adventure.)

Take the First Step

All this can feel overwhelming. Learning how to operate anything new—a new phone, a new appliance, or a new computer—takes time, energy, and most of all, patience. But after reading the instruction manual and applying what you've read, eventually, it starts to click. Sometimes we have to call in the experts for additional support. Know that I am here for you. We are going to take it line by line, slow and steady, in order to learn how to use the tools in our daily lives. I've selected those that have proven most helpful to clients and hope you find them helpful too. Hopefully my story informs your story, and ultimately your story will inform someone else's story. I want to help you help yourself because I know you possess wisdom and courage—two of the most important qualities needed in the process of transformation. Oh, they might be buried under a layer of lies, but they are there. I know it.

When I first started writing this book, I didn't realize that I, too, was going to be gutted, taken clear down to my own good bones. Walls have come down. Triggers have been exposed. Faulty thinking has been electrically rewired in my brain. It's been so much harder than I originally anticipated. But it has been good. I found myself sharing a more personal story than I planned to, but I believe it might be helpful.

Strength Training for the Soul

Today's Heartlift: "When you give yourself to places, they give you yourself back; the more one comes to know them, the more one seeds them with the invisible crop of memories and associations that will be waiting for you when you come back, while new places offer up new thoughts, new possibilities. Exploring the world is one of the best ways of exploring the mind, and walking travels both terrains."

Rebecca Solnit, *Wanderlust: A History of Walking*[6]

53

Envision: A Time to Think

Ancient Chinese Philosopher Lao Tzu adds this thought: "Do the difficult things while they are easy and do the great things while they are small. A journey of a thousand miles must begin with a single step."[7] As you start your Stronger Every Day journey, you take the first step on the path of *eudaimonia*.

Positive psychology is defined as "a field of psychological theory and research that focuses on the psychological states (e.g., contentment, joy), individual traits or character strengths (e.g., intimacy, integrity, altruism, wisdom), and social institutions that enhance subjective well-being and make life most worth living."[8] Cofounder Mihaly Csikszentmihalyi developed a theory of flow that details ways to achieve an optimal state of performance—flow—which is a key component in *eudaimonia*. He writes, "The best moments in our lives are not the passive, receptive, relaxing times. . . . The best moments usually occur if a person's body or mind is stretched to its limits in a voluntary effort to accomplish something difficult and worthwhile."[9] As you consider these eight characteristics of flow, envision how you might apply them:

1. Complete concentration on the task. *I commit to becoming stronger every day.*
2. Clarity of goals and reward in mind and immediate feedback. *As I apply and practice the nine tools, I will find more meaning, more purpose, and more joy.*
3. Transformation of time (speeding up/slowing down of time). *At times this journey might feel accelerated; and at other times, very slow and frustrating. I embrace both.*
4. The experience is intrinsically rewarding, is an end in itself. *True change happens from the inside out.*

5. Effortlessness and ease. *With God's help, I overcome.*

6. Balance between challenge and skills. *I set reasonable goals for myself.*

7. Actions and awareness are merged, losing self-conscious rumination. *I experience flow and deep satisfaction right now.*

8. A feeling of control over the task. *I am confident and secure in this process. When my heart is overwhelmed, God is present to help.*[10]

A Little "Envision" Bonus: For years, I've held on to the following powerful story. Known only as the February 9 entry in the classic devotional *Streams in the Desert*, it captures the immense wisdom of pursuing meaningfulness and illustrates beautifully the essence of human flourishing. Something tells me it is going to bless you too and that, like me, you will hold on to it for years.

Listen to an old and beautiful story of how one Christian dreamed that she saw three others at prayer. As they knelt the Master drew near to them.

As He approached the first of the three, He bent over her in tenderness and grace, with smiles full of radiant love and spoke to her in accents of purest, sweetest music. Leaving her, He came to the next, but only placed His hand upon her bowed head, and gave her one look of loving approval. The third woman He passed almost abruptly without stopping for a word or glance.

The woman in her dream said to herself, "How greatly He must love the first one, to the second He gave His approval, but none of the special demonstrations of love He gave the first; and the third must have grieved Him deeply, for He gave her no word at all and not even a passing look.

"I wonder what she has done, and why He made so much difference between them?" As she tried to account for the action of her Lord, He Himself stood by her and said: "O woman! how wrongly hast thou interpreted Me. The first kneeling woman needs all the weight of My tenderness and care to keep her feet in My narrow way. She needs My love, thought and help every moment of the day. Without it she would fail and fall.

"The second has stronger faith and deeper love, and I can trust her to trust Me however things may go and whatever people do. The third, whom I seemed not to notice, and even to neglect, has faith and love of the finest quality, and her I am training by quick and drastic processes for the highest and holiest service.

"She knows Me so intimately, and trusts Me so utterly, that she is independent of words or looks or any outward intimation of My approval. She is not dismayed nor discouraged by any circumstances through which I arrange that she shall pass; she trusts Me when sense and reason and every finer instinct of the natural heart would rebel;—because she knows that I am working in her for eternity, and that what I do, though she knows not the explanation now, she will understand hereafter."[11]

I offer this story at the beginning of your journey and invite you to tuck it away for safekeeping. There will be days ahead when you might feel as though you've been overlooked by God. Rest assured that he sees you. When "every finer instinct of the natural heart" tells you to quit your emotional healing journey, please remember this story and keep moving forward.

Educate: A Time to Learn

Adding to our conversation is the naturalist and philosopher Henry David Thoreau, whose famed essay "Walking" states, "The genius of walking lies not in mechanically putting one foot in front of the other en route to a destination but in mastering the art of sauntering."[12] *Sauntering.* Haven't heard that word in a while? To saunter is "to walk in a slow and relaxed way."[13] *Slow and relaxed.* Today, we don't often associate those two words with our idea of walking. Most of us hold to the idea of a good, solid "power walk." Burn calories, build muscle, and check it off the daily to-do list. Nothing wrong with that, but what if we took the wise advice of Thoreau in order to pursue meaningfulness? Dedicate at least one or two walks a week to practice the art of sauntering—in order to gain mental and emotional clarity. In my life, I consider it meditation in motion. Here is a simple approach:

1. Block one hour of time to saunter, sit, and see.
2. Saunter a bit.
3. Sit on a park bench, under a tree, next to a lake, or maybe on your own front porch.
4. See the landscape around you.
5. Take mental snapshots. What do you see? Notice the wind in the trees, a butterfly flitting from bush to bush, a snake slithering across the street (yes, I saw this just yesterday).
6. Pick up your pen and write a short, vivid description of your mental snapshot.
7. Be present and let this soul-nourishing practice settle deep within.
8. Meet me on Facebook or Instagram, @janellrardon, and post your mental snapshot. Let's encourage one another to saunter, sit, and see.

Establish: A Time to Build

In the establish sections, we will practice the spiritual discipline of meditation. One of my favorite thoughts on meditation comes from the English clergyman Thomas Manton (1620–77). He writes, "Meditation is a middle sort of duty between word and prayer and hath respect to both. The word feedeth meditation, and meditation feedeth prayer. These duties must go hand in hand; meditation must follow hearing and precede prayer. To hear and not to meditate is unfruitful. We may hear and hear, but it is like putting a thing into a bag with holes."[14] *A bag with holes.* His words and imagery have stayed with me for a long time. Simply put, meditation is holy thought, taking time to consider what God is saying to our hearts. Meditate on these beautiful passages from God's powerful message to us.

Today's Heartlifting Meditation	How Does This Relate to Living into *Eudaimonia*—Your Meaningful New Story?
Genesis 13:17 (AMP): "Arise, walk (make a thorough reconnaissance) around in the land, through its length and its width, for I will give it to you." To help you get started, consider the words within the word *reconnaissance*: "A preliminary survey to gain information; especially: an exploratory military survey of enemy territory."[15]	1. What two spiritual directives and one spiritual promise are given in this profound word from God to Abraham after his separation from Lot? Read Genesis 13 for more about this powerful story. 2. Take a mental "walk"—a thorough reconnaissance—around your life. In boldness (Heb. 4:16), ask God for insights, strategies, and information that might help you fight any existing "enemies" that might be in your "land."

TOOL 2

Sit in God's Presence

SECURE ATTACHMENT

THE INTENTION OF TOOL 2:
I sit in God's presence and feel safe and secure.

When we are in pain, when we can't see a way out, when the days drag by without solutions, he comes to us with tenderness and incredible love. This Gardener can take any branch, no matter how wounded, and put it back together again. It may not be a quick fix. It may take a while, but the Father has grace enough to forgive our failures and strength enough to transform any crisis. This is my Father's vineyard. He's in charge. He cares for us deeply and tenderly. He provides everything we need to grow and be fruitful. Isn't that a Gardener you can trust?

Wayne Jacobsen, *In My Father's Vineyard*

As I opened my front door, there stood a beautiful young family—husband, wife, and charming, adorable three-year-old daughter. This being their first time in my home, little Nora—a bit nervous and unsure—wrapped her chubby toddler arms around her mama's leg, clinging for dear life. Nothing and no one was going to pry her away from her safe place.

Within the hour, after sensing my home was also a safe place, Nora began venturing a few steps away from mom. She'd come a bit closer to me, give me a little glance, hand me a board book to read, and then scurry back to mom's leg, coy smile on her face. This little game lasted for quite some time, but by the end of the day, Nora nestled into my lap, relaxed and comfortable, allowing me to read a book to her.

This phenomenon is what psychologists and counselors call "secure attachment."[1] I began learning about attachment styles when my three children flew far from the nest—leaving me lost in the trauma of this normal parenting transition. From Virginia, one flew to the other side of the world, one to Kansas, and the other to St. Louis, Missouri. As I blogged about this parenting milestone, men and women would comment, "They must really be secure." I heard it over and over again. And many added, "You and Rob did a good job, Janell."

Why does everyone keep saying this? I'd ask myself. *What on earth does "being secure" have to do with leaving home and going so far away? I don't get it. And why does that mean we did a "good job"?*

Midway through an attachment and trauma certification program, I learned the answer to this agitating, yet intriguing, question.

Patterns Are Mental Models

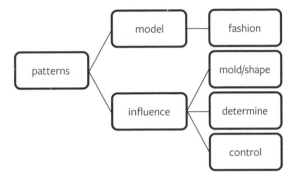

Licensed psychologist Hal Shorey writes:

About 55% of people emerge from childhood with secure attachment styles. Attachment styles are the building blocks of our personalities. They are like mental roadmaps that help us understand and predict how the environment and other people are likely to react to us in different situations. Through helping predict how people and the environment are likely to react, they also help us prepare mentally and emotionally to cope with whatever comes our way. Because these patterns of perceiving, understanding, and coping with the environment are practiced so many times across our early childhood years and into adulthood, they become automatic processes that are ingrained, not only in our thoughts and behaviors, but in the very structures of our brains and emotional systems.[2]

Shorey speaks of one very important word—*pattern*. His thought bears repeating: "Because these patterns of perceiving, understanding, and coping with the environment are practiced many times across our early childhood years and into adulthood, they become automatic processes." And, as a result, they ultimately settle into our "emotional systems." Parents help children organize and regulate these patterns, which become ingrained, automatic neural processes. They settle into the emotional fabric of a child's soul. When children are cared for by trustworthy, capable, empathic, and loving parents (and I like to add, imperfect, yet committed to emotional health and wellness), the children develop a remarkable capacity to expand their horizons and explore the world. When and if something unforeseen or difficult happens, they know they always have a secure home base—a safe place where they feel loved and, most importantly, valued.

Nothing, absolutely nothing, is more important than secure attachment. It sets the course of living an emotionally healthy, meaningful life.

Aha! Finally, I understood why people were telling us we raised secure children. The light bulb went on in my brain. Because my husband and I had provided our children with a home base steeped in a sense of security and safety, albeit imperfectly—being human and having both come from family backgrounds of alcoholism— our children emerged into adulthood with this great gift of secure attachment.

When Nature Speaks to Us

Nature parallels life. When I need a life lesson, I typically turn to God's creative work in nature. I've done this from a very young age, often wondering why I feel closer to God when surrounded by mountains, walking on the beach, riding my red Huffy, or caring for the plants in my yard. Often, I beat myself up a bit for feeling this way. *Shouldn't I feel closest to God in church? At a Bible study? While reading the Bible?* But one day, I read author Gary Thomas's book *Sacred Pathways: Discover Your Soul's Path to God*, in which he outlines "nine spiritual temperaments that God creates in human beings so that we can connect and worship him in unique ways."[3]

I was relieved to discover that, as what Thomas calls a naturalist, I love God *best* outdoors. He writes, "Naturalists have found that getting outside can actually flood parched hearts and soften the hardest soul. . . . It should be obvious, though modern conveniences hid the truth from me for so long, that the Bible is meant to be read outside. Many Old Testament and Gospel illustrations and allusions are based on nature, and it is only in the context of nature that they regain their meaning and force."[4]

As I write this chapter, it is summer here in Virginia. I'm sitting on my back porch, nestled comfortably under our cobalt blue patio umbrella, writing—each and every word bathed in late-afternoon sunshine. In Thomas's words, "The lessons we learn out of doors are waiting for us every day—a whole new cast coming to town with each changing season."[5]

Meet the new cast of my summer writing season. With great, ceremonious anticipation, I await the arrival of today's surprising Suffolk sunset. As I listen to the varied harmonious songs of my backyard birds—goldfinches, robins, doves, cardinals, bluebirds, and red-winged blackbirds—warm summer breezes blow across my rectangular glass-topped patio table. I've done my best to create a little paradise in which to entertain and to enjoy summer's bounty. Summer comes and goes so quickly here in Virginia that we have to be very intentional about seizing this sacred time. I've surrounded the brick patio with charming Spanish pots filled with bright-red geraniums; dazzling dahlias; big, blooming hydrangeas; and vines . . . lots and lots of vines—my favorite being the moonflower vine.

An Unassuming Little Seed

I first read of the mysterious moonflower vine in Jan Karon's *The Trellis and the Seed*. Karon weaves a warm tale about a woman called "Nice Lady" and her garden. Nice Lady loves flowers. At the end of summer, a friend hands her an unassuming little seed, off-white in color with wrinkled skin covering its outer shell. She tells Nice Lady that one day it will become "a beautiful vine with sweet-smelling blossoms."[6] The very ordinary small seed, now taking on the human quality of listening, homes in on the conversation and becomes the main character in the story. Overhearing this prophetic statement, Little Seed responds with disbelief and amazement: "How can I ever become a beautiful vine with sweet-smelling blossoms?" As if to say, *that is impossible. Look at me. Small. Shriveled. Certainly, no blossom can come of me.* After being shelved for the winter, Little Seed is painfully notched with Nice Lady's small kitchen paring knife, placed in a cup of water, and set to soak. Nice Lady buys a fancy white trellis and yes, you guessed it, plants Little Seed at the base of the trellis. There, inside a very dark, very cold hole, surrounded by rich, fertile soil, Little Seed waits—seemingly forgotten, desperately fearful, and soaked by torrential rain.

Time passes. It seems like years to Little Seed. Nice Lady visits every now and then, watering and fertilizing and encouraging Little Seed to do the impossible—climb the trellis! Finally, after what seems a lifetime, Little Seed experiences its own heartlift—it begins to twist this way and turn that way, securely attaching to the beautiful trellis. It can't stop itself from climbing higher and higher. Soon it forgets about all its discomforts—the darkness, the cold, the freezing rain. It's scared at first, of course, as everything is so new.

Little Seed isn't used to such freedom.

Much to its surprise, it soon becomes this remarkable, verdant, flourishing vine.

After a few days, though, it notices something very peculiar. Every single flower around it is blooming, but it remains bloomless, *until* . . .

Born to Cling, Born to Bloom

It pains me to leave you hanging on the vine (pun intended), but I must. If you want to know what happens to the moonflower vine, you must pick up a copy of the book and find out for yourself. Spoiler alert: it is a very happy ending.

I tried for years to plant and grow the annual moonflower in my backyard but met with only failure. I couldn't figure out what I was doing wrong, until my husband and I spent a day at the famed Maymont Estate in Richmond, Virginia, about an hour and a half from our home. Little did I know that I would stumble across master gardeners Keith and Melanie, who just so happened to have moonflower vines for sale.

"Moonflowers!" I shouted. "Rob, they have moonflower vines!"

"I've tried to grow these for years," I shared. "They just don't make it. What am I doing wrong?"

"Oh, moonflower vines are tricky," Keith said. "They rot easily. You have to notch them and soak them in water for a bit. Even when you handle them carefully, they are still at high risk for rotting in the ground. That is why we start the vines for you each year. You'll have a much better chance at them growing this way. One thing is for sure, they are born to cling and born to bloom! I can tell you are going to enjoy them."

I bought several and off I went. I couldn't wait to get my little vines home. I was more hopeful than ever, thanks to the wisdom and expertise of Keith and Melanie. A few days later, I stood in my backyard and, like Nice Lady, looked around for the perfect spot for each moonflower vine. Upon assessing our backyard, I chose a quiet little spot by the iron fence on the back of our property. I dug a hole, added some fertilizer and potting soil, lovingly planted the little vine, and watered it for safekeeping.

Filled with hope, I spoke a gardening prayer and smiled.

Grow, little vine, grow. I can't wait to see you blossom! You were born to cling and born to bloom. Now go and do what you've been born to do!

Secure Attachment = The Power of a Good Cling

Little Nora and Little Seed have something very important in common. They both understand secure attachment or, as I like to call it, "the power of a good cling." In order to climb higher in life and bloom into all God created them to be, they have to cling like crazy—that is, securely attach themselves to a strong, healthy support system. One of the most powerful of all "support systems" is found in the sixty-six books of the Bible. I turn to them first because "no word from God will ever fail" (Luke 1:37 NIV). To help you get started, I've chosen three powerful passages that helped me see "the power of a good cling."

For Little Nora, it was her mother and father.

For Little Seed, it was the strong trellis prepared by Nice Lady.

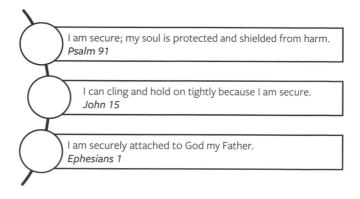

I am secure; my soul is protected and shielded from harm.
Psalm 91

I can cling and hold on tightly because I am secure.
John 15

I am securely attached to God my Father.
Ephesians 1

For you and for me, it is the loving, strong embrace of God, our heavenly Father.

Like me at one time, you may have no idea what "the loving, strong embrace of God" means. Early in my walk of faith, imagining God as Father was painfully difficult. I didn't have a strong, dependable father. The bottle won out most days. He seemed weak and worn. His addiction lured him away from being present as a parent. He was a good man; he just had a great big problem with alcohol. Thankfully, as I wrote in my first book, *Rock-Solid Families*, my father and I had a beautiful reconciliation before he passed.[7] For that, I am most grateful.

Making Sense of Your Story

The ramifications of my father's emotional absence (and a few other factors) left me with insecure attachment or anxious-avoidant attachment, one of the major styles of attachment. John Bowlby, known for his pioneering work in the field of attachment theory, describes attachment as "a deep and enduring emotional bond that connects one person to another across time and space."[8] A significant factor to keep in mind is the "across time and space" part of secure attachment. To simplify, think of attachment style and how that relates to the "good bones"—that is, the construction of a house:

- Secure attachment: The good bones of this house are solid, safe, and built on a secure foundation. Matthew 7:24–25 describes this house as one built on a rock. Rain, wind, and storms will come, but nothing will destroy this house. Members of the family who live here trust and believe that no matter what may come, they will be okay (Rom. 8:28). They have a very strong sense of ME + YOU = SECURE, SAFE WE.

- Insecure (anxious-avoidant or anxious-ambivalent) attachment: Imagine a house built with no locks on the windows and doors. It isn't safe and secure from harm. The kind-of-good bones of this house leave family members unsure of their safety. They might have to look outside of the house for other ways to be safe and secure. They have a sense of ME + YOU = INSECURE, MAYBE UNSAFE WE.

- Disorganized/Disordered attachment: This is a no-good-bones house. Matthew 7:26–27 describes this as a house built on sand. Rain, wind, and storms will cause this house to fall. Family members do not feel safe, secure, or stable and will have to either fend for themselves or look outside the home for a sense of safety, which often is maladaptive. They have the sense of ME + YOU = DYS-FUNCTIONAL, UNSTABLE, UNSAFE WE.

When I first learned about attachment styles (secure, anxious-avoidant/anxious-ambivalent, disorganized/disordered), I couldn't get enough. Like Little Seed, I couldn't stop myself from climbing higher and higher on the vine of self-discovery—studying, reading, and getting postgraduate certifications to know more. One overarching truth fueled my discoveries: research has proven that no matter what our background, change can take place. We can obtain "earned secure attachment."[9] Earned secure adult attachment is possible when one or more of the following occur:

- A person commits to making sense of their story—taking the time and energy to pick up the pen and rewrite their personal history. Dan Siegel writes, "Attachment research demonstrates that the best predictor of a child's security of attachment is not what happened to his parents as children, but rather how his parents made sense of those childhood experiences. The key to 'making sense' of one's life experiences is to write a coherent narrative, which helps them understand how their childhood experiences are still affecting them in their life today. When one creates a coherent narrative, they actually rewire their brain to cultivate more security within themselves and their relationships."[10]

Can I hear a great big amen? Heartlifters, this is our purpose and mission: taking our personal and family history of hurts and transforming them into a vision of victory. Neuroplasticity, the brain's ability to reorganize itself by forming new neural connections throughout life,[11] affirms what we already know: changing the hard wiring in our brains is possible!

- A person forms an attachment with someone or others who have secure attachment. Change cannot happen *alone*; it happens *in relationship*. Lisa Firestone writes:

  One of the proven ways to change our attachment style is by forming an attachment with someone who had a more secure attachment style than what we've experienced. We can also talk to a therapist, as the therapeutic relationship can help create a more secure attachment. We can continue to get to know ourselves through understanding our past experiences, allowing ourselves to make sense and feel the full pain of our stories, then moving forward as separate, differentiated adults. In doing this, we move through the world with an internal sense of security that helps us better withstand the natural hurts that life can bring.[12]

- A person "attunes" or becomes "aware and receptive" to those around them.[13] In my practice, I refer to this emotional awakening as "having eyes to see." Emotional attunement, then, involves "being in harmony first with oneself, then with another, and finally with circumstances."[14] In simplest terms, attunement is "our ability to be present to, and with, another's expression of their experience."[15] One important goal of this book is to help you experience the power of a heartlift: become aware of your emotions, healthy and unhealthy, and ultimately learn to vocalize your pain in a safe manner that leads to your lasting freedom in Christ.

Secure in Your Father's Love

The reason we struggle with insecurity is because we compare our behind-the-scenes with everyone else's highlight reels.

Pastor Steve Furtick[16]

When Debbie walked into my office, her face said it all. Typically a joyful, buoyant young woman, today she seemed like she was carrying the weight of the world on her shoulders.

For about a month, we had been talking about attachment styles and Debbie's inability to overcome her battle with insecurity. As a single woman, she struggled with welcoming God into the whys of her singleness.

"Yesterday, I saw a friend's engagement announcement on Facebook," she said. "I had been doing so good. It had been an unusually long day of working, and I suppose I was really vulnerable. Funny how that happens, right?"

"Oh, Debbie," I said. "I am so sorry. I can only imagine how that triggered your deep desire to be married."

"Yes," she said, tears welling up in her eyes. "Those nasty, negative whispers started right in. *You must not be worthy of love. Still single at thirty-two years old?* Every single insecurity voice started talking in my head. I thought my brain would explode."

"Well then," I said, "let's talk back." I smiled and handed her a Kleenex.

Inside the Heart of (In)Security

Tim Clinton and Gary Sibcy, authors of *Why You Do the Things You Do*, help us see why Debbie reacted so strongly to her friend's post. "Soul wounds trigger intense, painful emotions, and too many people deal with this pain by burying it," they warn. "When we do this, these emotions—and the beliefs they foster about self and others—are mummified, locking us into negative, rigid views of how relationships work and how we should behave."[17]

Debbie's heart of gold and willingness to change led us to dissect the stronghold (Eph. 4:27) that insecurity—her soul wound—had on her life. First, we put the words *security* and *insecurity* side by side in order to examine them and better understand how insecurity might be a stronghold in her life:

Security, from Latin root *securitas*, "free from care."	Insecurity, from Latin root *insecuritas*, "unsafe."
• The state of being free from danger or threat.	• Uncertainty or anxiety about oneself; lack of confidence.
• The state of feeling safe, stable, and free from fear or anxiety.[18]	• The state of being open to danger or threat; lack of protection.[19]
Synonyms: certainty, safety, reliability, soundness, dependability.	Synonyms: self-doubt, unassertiveness, timidity, uncertainty, nervousness, worry, unease, instability, fragility, defenselessness.

Insecurity complicates and confuses. It makes our imaginations run wild. It creates hypersensitivity and discontent, and it is unhealthy. Very, very unhealthy. Left to itself, it leads to the even deeper issue of inferiority. Insecurity loves to get in the middle of our lives and mess with our minds. Up to this moment, Debbie was moving forward and living into her beautiful new story. Then, wham! Out of nowhere, which always seems to be the case, Debbie's insecurity was triggered, and she was taken off guard and sent whirling down the rabbit hole of anxiety and disconnection.

For just a few minutes, Debbie forgot that she had a shiny new tool kit filled with tools that would help her maintain emotional health and wellness.

"Debbie, you tell me what you need to do," I said. "We have talked about this."

She smiled. "In times like these, I need to transform insecurity into (IN)➔SECURITY." Then she sighed. "I need to remember that in Christ and Christ alone, I am secure. I have value, worth, and dignity, and when it is time, he will give me the desires of my heart."

Setbacks will happen. We will be taken off guard. We will momentarily forget the how-tos. We will fall down (Prov. 24:16). But with continued practice and the loving support of our Stronger Every Day community, we will press on toward the mark of the high calling in Christ Jesus (Phil. 3:14) and live into our beautiful, ever-increasingly meaningful new story.

Strength Training for the Soul

Today's Heartlift: "Unlike the vines in my Father's vineyard, which cannot defend themselves, we play a key role in resisting the enemy's hand by recognizing his attempts and refusing to fall victim to his lies. Whenever he tries to weaken our relationship to God, to distract us from simple obedience to God or discourage our efforts to show the fruits of the Spirit, we need not let him succeed. There is no doubt about the outcome when we cling to the friendship God has extended to us."

Wayne Jacobsen, *In My Father's Vineyard*[20]

Envision: A Time to Think

There is power in a good cling. We've talked a great deal about clinging, and so I want to be clear that we are talking about a *good* cling, not a *too-clingy* cling, which translates as codependency or insecurity or neediness in relationships.

Good Cling (Interdependence)	Too-Clingy Cling (Codependence)
Interdependence creates strong, healthy relationships. "An interdependent person recognizes the value of vulnerability, being able to turn to their partner in meaningful ways to create emotional intimacy. They also value a sense of self that allows them and their partner to be themselves without any need to compromise who they are or their values system."[21] In this relationship, me + you = we.	Codependence creates unhealthy, enmeshed relationships. "Codependent relationships are not healthy and do not allow partners room to be themselves, to grow and to be autonomous. These unhealthy relationships involve one partner, or both, relying heavily on the other and the relationship for their sense of self, feelings of worthiness and overall emotional well-being. There are often feelings of guilt and shame for one or both partners when the relationship is not going well."[22] In this relationship, me + you = confused we. I don't know where I end and you begin and where you begin and I end; no emotional/mental boundaries exist.

In true God-fashion, a lesson on *too much* cling unfolded before my eyes the second season I planted moonflower vines. After my first successful year of growing moonflowers, I asked my dear husband, Rob, to construct a special trellis just for these. So in the heat of a very humid Virginia afternoon, he built his precious wife a beautiful frame for her moonflowers. I planted one of the new vines on the left side and one on the right side. *Note: one vine on each side.* Within a month or so, they were off and climbing. And they kept climbing. Higher and higher and wider and wider.

By the end of the summer, we had a moonflower monster taking over our backyard.

I wish I could say it was pretty and that every night it brought me greater and greater joy. *It didn't.* It actually stressed me out and caused my husband even greater anxiety. For a man of order, the unruliness of the vines was just too much.

He gently asked me, repeatedly, one question: "When do you think you will take down the vines?"

And then, when fall was setting in, he asked one more time: "When do you think you will take the vines down?"

Overwhelmed by the thought of tackling all the clinging going on, I procrastinated—which is how I handle life issues I'd rather avoid—until one afternoon when he asked that question again.

I huffed. I puffed. I grabbed my gardening shears and gloves, along with the trash bin, and with a great deal of grumble and mumble, I dove in. What I found astounded me. Once again, nature became my wise mentor and offered a vivid illustration of enmeshment* in my own backyard.

So often in our family systems and relationships, we become overconcerned for one another, hyperconnected, and we lose a sense of autonomous development (more help on self-discovery is coming in Tool 3). One person doesn't know where they end and the other begins. There is way too much unhealthy clinging going on. In a healthy family system, there is just enough cling.

It took me hours to unwind and disentangle the tightly grasped cling of one vine to the other. They were clinging so tightly I thought I'd lose my mind. What began in a bit of anger and frustration ended in an eye-opening and deeply spiritual experience on what healthy clinging looks like.[23]

We've spent time sharpening this tool of secure attachment so that we can recognize any spaces and places in our hearts that lack this vital, healthy ability to cling well. Possessing secure attachment means we become resilient human beings who live from a place of spiritual strength and emotional stability—knowing that God, our heavenly Father, loves us unconditionally and that he watches over us as a caring, loving, protective father does. This deep, solid connection allows us to live into our God-created purpose and empowers us with emotional health and wellness, which ultimately lead to a rich, meaningful life.

Educate: A Time to Learn

Living in the age of distraction, I find I need simple, practical exercises to keep my mind focused on the task at hand. Can you relate? Using the acronym CLING, following are five prompts to help you write your new narrative and begin living your beautiful new story. Set aside some quiet time for this. Silence invites the Spirit to speak and move. *Listen for the Spirit's whispers.* Silence invites us to get to know our authentic, God-created self, to *connect to our core beliefs and values.* Ready? Pick up your pen and have fun.

- Consider secure attachment. What does this look like or feel like to you? After reviewing the attachment systems (www.janellrardon.com/resources) and taking the attachment quiz,[24] what attachment style do you have? Take some time to read about and reflect on it. How is your attachment style affecting your closest, most intimate relationships?
- Look at nature's reflection of the power of a good cling. If you don't have a vine growing on a trellis in your yard, visit a local botanical garden or search *vines* on the

internet. There are fascinating videos on how vines cling and grow. After watching, how do these video interpretations of clinging vines image your clinging to God? Do they offer any wisdom or advice on the power of a good cling?

• Identify where and what make you feel alive and fully awake. Generally, this will be a safe space in which you feel secure and stable. The Outer Banks of North Carolina, particularly Rodanthe, is one of those safe places for me. One of my clients, Gina, recalls the haymow on her family farm in Vermont. What is your special safe place? Read this short excerpt from *The Secret Garden* and perhaps re-create this experience for yourself: "The sun shone down for nearly a week on the secret garden. The Secret Garden was what Mary called it when she was thinking of it. She liked the name, and she liked still more the feeling that when its beautiful old walls shut her in no one knew where she was. It seemed almost like being shut out of the world in some fairy place."[25]

• Name negative influences, negative-feedback loops, and naysayers in your life. How might secure attachment—that is, clinging to God your Father—help you resist the urge to succumb to your own negative self-talk and avoid the downward spiral brought on by negative people? Take one example and rewind and reset by writing a new response. Note that negative self-talk often shows up in the seemingly silliest of events. See the following example. (I've been so tempted to change my example because it is hyper-silly, but time and time again, it is situations and circumstances like this that get the best of us.)

The Negative Influence: We hadn't been to church in a few weeks. Now that it was summertime, frequent weekend getaways kept us from attending services. Finally, we were in town and able to get to Sunday's contemporary service. Within minutes, several women commented to me, "Wow, look at you! So shiny! Those earrings. That shiny silver top. You don't normally wear such shiny clothes. Really different. You look like a Christmas ornament. So out of character to wear something so vintage-looking." Just an hour before, I had thrown together an outfit, not knowing what a stir it would cause. My original plan was to wear a simple dress, but I noticed a big spot and, due to time constraints, had to throw together another outfit. I chose a blouse I hadn't worn in years. It seems silly, I agree, but it ended up causing a bit of a stir in my soul. When I returned home, I immediately shamed myself: *What were you thinking? Why did you wear that? Obviously, not the right choice. Tone it down, already.*

The Rewind and Reset: I said to myself, *Janell, really? This mental mind game is immature, unhealthy, and honestly, quite ridiculous. Are you really going to let a shiny silver blouse control your emotional health and wellness? It is a blouse, for heaven's sake!*

Isn't it crazy how we let silly things get to us? Typically, this is where triggers ignite, stealing our joy and robbing us of rest. We give insecurity permission to wreak havoc on our stability and contentment.

- Gather strength from healthy relationships and community. Healing doesn't happen in isolation. Brené Brown writes:

True belonging is not passive. It's not the belonging that comes with just joining a group. It's not fitting in or pretending or selling out because it's safer. [True belonging] is a practice that requires us to be vulnerable, get uncomfortable, and learn how to be present with people without sacrificing who we are. If we are going to change what is happening in a meaningful way, we're going to need to intentionally be with people who are different from us. We're going to have to sign up and join and take a seat at the table. We're going to have to learn how to listen, have hard conversations, look for joy, share pain, and be more curious than defensive, all while seeking moments of togetherness.[26]

Stop right now and join our online community at www .janellrardon.com. Come and take a seat at our table.

Establish: A Time to Build

Read through Romans 8:31–39 several times.

What would we say about all of this? If God is on our side, *then tell me:* whom should we fear? If He did not spare His own Son, but handed Him over on our account, then don't you think that He will graciously give us all things with Him? Can anyone be so bold as to level a charge against God's chosen? Especially since God's "not guilty" verdict is already declared. Who has the authority to condemn? Jesus the Anointed who died, but more importantly, conquered death when He was raised to sit at the right hand of God where He pleads on our behalf. So, who can separate us? What can come between us and the love of God's Anointed? Can troubles, hardships, persecution, hunger, poverty, danger, or even death? The answer is, absolutely nothing. As the psalm says, "On Your behalf, our lives are endangered constantly; we are like sheep awaiting slaughter." But no matter what comes, we will always taste victory through Him who loved us. For I have every confidence that nothing—not death, life, heavenly messengers, *dark* spirits, the present, the future, spiritual powers, height, depth, nor any created thing—can come between us and the love of God revealed in the Anointed, Jesus our Lord.

Meditation: What do these words say to you? Do they inspire hope and promise? Do they seem impossible and out of reach? In your journal, write freely about what comes to your mind.

TOOL 3

Shape Healthy Thoughts

COGNITIVE REFRAMING

THE INTENTION OF TOOL 3:
I shape healthy thoughts each and every day.

The Secret Garden was what Mary called it when she was thinking of it. She liked the name, and she liked still more the feeling that when its beautiful old walls shut her in, no one knew where she was. It seemed almost like being shut out of the world in some fairy place. The few books she had read and liked had been fairy-story books, and she had read of secret gardens in some of the stories. Sometimes people went to sleep in them for a hundred years, which she had thought must be rather stupid. She had no intention of going to sleep, and, in fact, she was becoming wider awake every day which passed at Misselthwaite.

Frances Hodgson Burnett, *The Secret Garden*

When I first read Burnett's *The Secret Garden*, I felt sheer magic. She takes an old forgotten, overgrown, somewhat mysterious garden, places a broken-hearted little girl inside of it, and together, they find a new life filled with flourishing beauty.

Gardens invite us to come in and sit for a spell. They awaken our childhood senses. At least, they have that effect on me. Within minutes, I'm spellbound, like Mary at Misselthwaite Manor, peering around corners, picking up stones, and imagining fairies living under the broad umbrella of wild mushrooms.

Perhaps one of the most powerful sentences in *The Secret Garden* is when the narrator shares that Mary "had no intention of going to sleep, and, in fact, she was becoming wider awake every day which passed."

I know exactly how Mary feels.

Wider Awake Every Day

Sometimes our path in life is strewn with hard times. We walk through some tough places. Some last longer than others. Some entangle us so tightly we can hardly breathe. Some are brief yet bully us beyond belief. Some come in like a thief in the night—rest robbers who steal our joy as well. Some shake us to the core, like an unexpected earthquake. But then, right when you think you could sleep for a hundred years, you realize, *I don't want to go to sleep*. In fact, you realize you have absolutely no intention of going to sleep because you feel wider awake than ever.

That is how I felt yesterday.

I escaped to my own secret garden, known to the rest of Virginia as *Lavender Field Farms*. I wanted to learn more about the process of growing different varieties of lavender. My husband and I had experimented with a few plants in our flowerbeds. Some did well; some failed miserably. I was on a mission to learn how to plant and care for this fragrant plant. While walking the grounds, smelling and learning about all the different types of lavender, I saw their yearly calendar and noted an herbal-wreath-making class being held during the farm's upcoming fall festival. I decided right then and there that I was coming back to make my own herbal wreath. *What a great way to collect strength in my soul.*

I was right. A few months later, my friend Gail and I took a Saturday morning road trip and found ourselves wider awake than ever. For two and a half hours, our wise teacher, Nicole, owner of the beloved farm, led us on a tour. As we wandered through the opulent gardens, she shared botanical facts about this plant and that flower, instructing us on the best ones to use for our wreaths. She then invited us to select any of the foliage and flowers we wanted. With wicker baskets nestled in the crook of our arms, we clipped here and there and everywhere. Later, we learned how to weave and arrange them into lovely herbal wreaths.

I couldn't stop smiling. The day held its own extraordinary magic. The sun was shining, the bees were buzzing, the plants and herbs were in full array, and women were learning, creating, laughing, and—for a few minutes—forgetting about everything else in life. That's what I call a "wider-awake" kind of day.

Our Minds Are Like a Garden

One of the world's earliest self-help authors, James Allen, in his classic book, *As a Man Thinketh*, wisely compared the mind to a garden. Biographers give insights into why he might have come to this conclusion. When he was fifteen, his father was robbed and murdered. Allen had to quit school and go to work to support his family. This childhood trauma forced him to grow up quickly and face difficult grown-up challenges. Perhaps that is why, later in life, he decided to leave the hustle and bustle of city life and move to the countryside, where he could live a simpler, more contemplative life. He writes:

> A man's mind may be likened to a garden, which may be intelligently cultivated or allowed to run wild; but whether cultivated or neglected, it must, and will, bring forth. If no useful seeds are put into it, then an abundance of useless weed seeds will fall therein and will continue to produce their kind. . . . By pursuing this process, a man sooner or later discovers that he is the master-gardener of his soul, the director of his life. He also reveals, within himself, the laws of thought, and understands with ever-increasing accuracy, how the thought-forces and mind elements operate in the shaping of his character, circumstances, and destiny.[1]

Allen's words sound as if they could be commentary on the apostle Paul's words found in his final exhortation to the church at Philippi. Might he have been a student of Paul's writings? I can't find evidence of any such correlation, but his words echo the wisdom of Philippians 4:8: "Finally, believers, whatever is true, whatever is honorable and worthy of respect, whatever is right and confirmed by God's word, whatever is pure and wholesome, whatever is lovely and brings peace, whatever is admirable and of good repute; if there is any excellence, if there is anything worthy of praise, think continually on these things [center your mind on them, and implant them in your heart]" (AMP).

Cognitive Reframing 101

Both Paul's and Allen's words herald the potential and power of the seeds of our thought life. They also present us with two clear choices: either we cultivate the mind, or we neglect it. In the mental health field, cognition* is defined by the American Psychological Association as "all forms of knowing and awareness, such as perceiving, conceiving, remembering, reasoning, judging, imagining, and problem solving. Along with affect and conation, it is one of the three traditionally identified components of mind."[2]

Cognition is a fancy word for our thoughts and our thought processes.

- Why do we think the way we think?
- Why do we hear the way we hear?
- Why do we speak to others the way we do?
- Why do we allow others to speak to us the way they do?[3]

Our answers to these four questions often reveal important information about something called cognitive distortion*—or faulty thinking—known in some circles as "stinkin' thinkin',"[4] irrational ways of processing our thoughts that cloud the skies of mental clarity or simple, clear thinking. I like the simplicity of the *Cambridge Dictionary*'s definition of stinking thinking: "a bad way of thinking that makes you believe you will fail, that bad things will happen to you, or that you are not a very good person."[5] Where do these distortions come from? Are they a product of nature or nurture or both?

- Sometimes we are born with natural bents toward thinking and behaving in a certain way, often based on genetic disposition and cultural influence.[6] *Perfectionists are hard on themselves. Pessimists see the glass half empty. Passionate individuals lean toward being hot-tempered. Introverts tend to retreat. Extroverts tend to overshare.*

- Sometimes our family of origin* shapes or "nurtures" patterns of faulty thinking. *Children of alcoholics lean toward codependency. Dissatisfied mothers live through a child, often creating enmeshment. High achievers lean toward ambition and striving. Anxious parents often create fear-based tendencies.*

- Sometimes life throws us hard times, and our thinking gets muddled. *Bullied children often withdraw, isolate, or become aggressive. Sudden losses and unexpected circumstances dampen and depress. Sexual abuse steals innocence and trust. Traumatic medical diagnoses cause confusion, fear, and heightened anxiety.*

- Sometimes great success and ease breed entitlement. *Some people believe they are invincible, that nothing or no one will get in their way, and that they deserve to be spoken to and treated in a certain way, despite their actions.*

- Sometimes authoritarian households (as well as churches, schools, and organizations) stifle or repress our thinking. *Some people believe they have no voice, their needs don't matter, nobody cares about them, and they'll never measure up.*

- Sometimes neglect or abuse leaves us shamed and shattered. *Some people believe they will never be good enough, so why should they even try? They feel worthless.*

Whatever the case, God's design for our minds, as Paul so beautifully described, is for our thinking to be healthy and whole.

Is it possible, then, in light of these cognitive distortions in our minds—and the million ways they work—to be healthy and highly functional? Yes, absolutely! Tool 3 is all about reframing our cognitive processes. It helps us to observe and note where unhealthy thoughts—that is, irrational, illogical, or ill-fitting thoughts—occur in our lives, *and* it helps us to discern the motives behind the automatic and emotional reactions we tend to have to those thoughts.

Depending on the school of thought, examples of cognitive distortion vary. For the sake of ease of use, I've compiled a list of the top ten[7] and given them nicknames that will help us remember them:

1. The Assumer: cognition based on assumption; we think we know what someone else is thinking. *She thinks I am stupid. He hates me. They don't like me.*

2. The Magnifier: blowing things way out of proportion. *My husband bounced a check; our credit rating is completely ruined.*

3. The Shrinker: denial of how something affected us. *It's really no big deal. No worries. My story is silly compared to the suffering of others.*

4. The Generalizer: conclusion based on one or two events that are then taken as a universal law. *I was emotionally wounded in a church setting. All churches are unsafe, and I'll never go back to church.* Universal statements include the words *all, never, everyone, always*—for example, *You never answer my texts. You always do that.*

5. The Black-and-White Thinker: thinking in absolutes. *Either I do it right or I don't do it at all. I failed once at it; I will always fail at it. I burned the first meal in my marriage; therefore, I am an awful cook.*

6. The Judger: preconceived notions and expectations of others; "shoulding"[8] everyone. *You should discipline your children this way. You should call me every day. You should think this way.*

7. The Personalizer: takes everything personally; everything is our fault, whether this is true or not. *Her mean words are because I did something wrong.*

8. The Discounter: seeing only the negative and discounting anything positive. *Someone compliments you and immediately you respond, "I could have done better."*

9. The Labeler: both applying words or phrases onto others and believing words or phrases placed on us by others. *She is the messy daughter. He doesn't know how to tell time; he's always late. He always was the class clown.*

10. The Emotionalist: allowing emotions to rule our perceptions and interpretations. *If I feel this way, it must be true. I wasn't picked for the team. They hate me. I am a loser.*

Have you ever wished there was a mental gym where you could work out unhealthy thoughts? You might consider a therapy session with a professional counselor or psychiatrist as a mental gym. Life coaching, spiritual direction, inner work, and self-help can also provide workouts for your thinking.

What about something you could use in between these types of sessions or on your own, something that would give you a "mental" workout? I created a tool for my clients called "heartlifting"*—

a mindful program for reframing cognitive distortions. First, I needed to try it out and see if it had potential. For twenty-one days, the average time it takes to create a new habit, I kept a chart, much like you'd do for a new diet or exercise regimen, noting five significant factors:

1. Date and time of faulty thinking (that stinkin' thinkin' mentioned before).
2. Trigger word, phrase, nonverbal action, or event.
3. Emotional response. *How did the unhealthy thought make me feel—in my emotions? Why did it agitate me? If it angered me, why the anger? If it shamed me, why the shame? If it shut me down, why the shutdown?*
4. Automatic thought: the one that immediately pops into mind when triggered; the go-to reaction or feedback loop, which typically isn't a healthy response. It is critical to recognize and note the first thought that pops into mind. Don't judge it, try to push it away, or analyze it. Often-times it has a sarcastic, harsh, judging tone. Go with the first thought, even if it doesn't make any sense to you. Your subconscious is speaking to you.
5. Reframed thought: the one that reframes the thought into a healthy one. I encourage my clients to use their "intention setting" skills here, creating a one-sentence intention that is positive, first person, and present tense. For example, "I only speak healing words about myself."

Within minutes, and I mean minutes, of starting my own heart-lifting program, a trigger event occurred.

There Will Be Bad Days

Not thirty minutes after a fabulous, challenging, life-giving church service, I found myself in my local superstore tempted to be mean.

There, I said it. Put me in the corner; I deserve a time-out. I'm not proud of myself, but I must be completely honest with you.

The cashier checked me out without *ever* looking at me, greeting me, or even acting like I was standing in front of her. *Nothing rattles me, an Enneagram 2 (social subtype), like ignoring my presence.*[9] It triggers roots of rejection and disapproval. My husband witnessed it all, so I know I am not crazy.

Usually, I will do whatever it takes to win over the hardest of hearts (or at least try), but this cashier, wearing a bright-pink breast cancer awareness T-shirt, didn't budge. She wasn't giving me an inch. My theory that a little kindness soothes anything was null and void.

Usually, I try to put myself in the other person's shoes, considering that maybe they've had a rough day—even a rough life. Because of my profession, I know this is highly possible.

Usually, I am empathic and practice being kinder than I feel. But on this particular day, her behavior triggered something deep inside of me. I couldn't grasp any of my own emotional-health tools. I reacted and let anger get the best of me.

While growling, grimacing, and grunting (all on the inside, of course, since repression is my go-to defense mechanism*), my husband and I silently walked to the car.

"Let it go, Janell, it's not worth the energy," my husband said. "Just let it go."

"Ugh. Is it really that hard to be kind?" I replied. "She acted like we were invisible. Really?"

Most of the time, when I find myself in front of someone like that cashier, I ask how they are doing, but for some odd reason I didn't this time. I like to give people the benefit of the doubt because most of the time people are just having a bad day. The Lord knows I've had more than my share of bad days.

But, in all honesty, she just seemed—unkind. Like she truly didn't care.

I think that is what really got to me. It really hurt my heart—well, frustrated my heart.

I couldn't let it go.

I wish I could tell you I bounced back quickly, but I didn't. It was the day after an emotionally charged news cycle, and I was tired. The entire world seemed tired. So instead of my normal be-kinder-than-you-feel self, I was disturbed for the rest of the day and continued to think about why her behavior had affected me so deeply.

More than anything, I hated the fact that I had failed the test and let her behavior inform my behavior. Let her bad day ruin my day. *I know better. This is my gig. Why couldn't I speak healing words in this situation?*

Ugh.

Applying Heartlifting to Our Thought Life

We won't get along with everyone. Sometimes, no matter what we do, there will be those we offend, those who don't like us. Something about us just doesn't click with them. You see, I'm not sure what offended my cashier. Maybe something about *me* triggered *her*. But there I go assuming again, which is one of my stinkin' thinkin' defaults.* Maybe my perception was skewed, and this was my unhealthy interpretation of the situation. I do know that my top cognitive distortions are being an Emotionalist and a Personalizer, so I try to practice awareness daily via the examen in any conflicts that come into my day. I have big emotions and tend to be hypersensitive—both evidence of my Enneagram 2 type (see "A Time to Learn" at the end of this chapter).

Later in the afternoon, my husband came alongside me and reminded me of these wise words: "Good sense and discretion make a man slow to anger. And it is his honor and glory to overlook a transgression or an offense [without seeking revenge and harboring resentment]" (Prov. 19:11 AMP).

This ancient proverb points to the heart of the matter. When this woman's nonverbal actions triggered me, I allowed them to fester—a very dangerous and emotionally unhealthy thing to do. Festering infers that there's an infection, which never leads to anything good. But because of my personal commitment to the threefold cord of emotional health and wellness—the journey that our Stronger Every Day community is committed to walking—I was determined to practice awareness, understand my agitation, and ultimately, address my initial reaction in hopes of reframing any and all cognitive distortions. In my work, I've expanded the concept of "let it go" by helping both my clients and me identify the *it*. What is the *it* I really need to let go of? This strategic identification process brings real change—from the inside out.

I created a heartlifting chart to get to the bottom of my reaction at the store and help me work through identifying the *it*. Here's how I worked through my Sunday saga:

Date/Time	Trigger Event	Initial Emotional Response	Automatic Thought	Reframed Thought
Cashier, Sunday after church	The nonverbal cues of ignoring, detachment, and lack of care and concern.	Anger	*How dare she? Isn't the customer always king?*	*There is more to this than meets the eye.*
	No eye contact. Disgusted look on face.	Personalization and Emotionalism	*What did you do to this woman? She doesn't like you. Stop thinking about yourself. You are so selfish.*	*Don't personalize. Everything isn't always your fault. Use emotion regulation and breathe. This isn't about you.*
	Feeling invisible and unliked.	Avoidance and Repression	*Don't address. Be nice. People are watching. It's no big deal. Get over yourself.*	*Let the woman have a bad day. She isn't hurting you. Pray for her.*

This might sound like a whole lot of work because it *is* a whole lot of work. I think that is why so many of us quit when the going gets tough. We lose steam and rightfully so. But please don't stop. You are standing on the threshold of a breakthrough. By identifying the root of your trigger(s), your *it*, you can let go, implement the new tools in your emotional-health tool kit, and move forward into a meaningful new story.

The beautiful reward at the finish line? Freedom.

The apostle Paul knew the power of perseverance. He, like me, wants all of us to cross the freedom finish line. He left us these words:

But whatever I used to count as my greatest accomplishments, I've written them off as a loss because of the Anointed One. And more so, I now realize that all I gained and thought was important was nothing but yesterday's garbage compared to knowing the Anointed Jesus my Lord. For Him I have thrown everything aside—it's nothing but a pile of waste—so that I may gain Him. When it counts, I want to be found belonging to Him, not clinging to my own righteousness based on law, but actively relying on the faithfulness of the Anointed One. This is true righteousness, supplied by God, acquired by faith. I want to know Him inside and out. I want to experience the power of His resurrection and join in His suffering, shaped by His death, so that I may arrive safely at the resurrection from the dead.

I'm not there yet, nor have I become perfect; but I am charging on to gain anything and everything the Anointed One, Jesus, has in store for me—and nothing will stand in my way because He has grabbed me and won't let me go. Brothers and sisters, as I said, I know I have not arrived; but there's one thing I am doing: I'm leaving my old life behind, putting everything on the line for this mission. I am sprinting toward the only goal that counts: to cross the line, to win the prize, and to hear God's call to resurrection life found exclusively in Jesus the Anointed. All of us who are mature ought to think the same way about these matters. If you have a different attitude, then God will reveal this to you as well. For now, let's hold on to what we have been shown and keep in step with these teachings. (Phil. 3:7–16)

Can you feel Paul's passion and urgency here? He is fired up! His passion pulsates through every word. He is desperate for each one of us to be free. And that freedom comes by "leaving my old life behind, putting everything on the line for this mission"—our mission of emotional health and wellness.

Out with the Old, In with the New

Stronger Every Day is all about proclaiming, "Out with the old, in with the new."

My old narrative? Little Miss People Pleaser.

My old narrative's unhealthy thought? I want everyone to like me, and I'll do whatever it takes to make someone like me.

My new narrative? Woman Clothed in Strength and Dignity (Prov. 31:25).

My new narrative's healthy thought? I am clothed in God's strength and dignity and now accept, love, and value the God-breathed "me," even when I am emotionally triggered.

My encounter with the cashier immediately activated old, unhealthy thoughts: *She doesn't like me, and I need her to like me.* When this happened, my negative-feedback loop started on automatic pilot:

My old narrative, Little Miss People Pleaser, kicked in, and I went out of my way to smile at her and be nice.

My very unhealthy old narrative pressed me to win her favor, but she never responded. Her refusal made me even angrier because she was seemingly rejecting me.

My serious root of rejection—that is, unresolved trauma stored in my amygdala—flared up. I've come a long way, but it can be alive and kicking on the inside. So, in my naivete—or maybe I wasn't naive at all—I believe God

orchestrated this entire Sunday saga to invite me to cultivate the garden of my mind.

Gardening and renovation share a common passion: see something neglected or worn and transform "the good bones" into
something beautiful. Our God does the same, and he does it out
of his love for us (Rom. 2:4).[10] Without question, we will meet
people every day who challenge us, rub us the wrong way, or maybe
just don't like us. As heartlifters, we accept this truth and do our
best not to take it personally, even when it feels personal. By co-
operating with the spirit of God and practicing our heartlifting
principles, we can and will be a beautiful fragrance (2 Cor. 2:15)
to ourselves and others and, in doing so, will make our spheres of
influence much healthier places to be.

Strength Training for the Soul

Today's Heartlift: "Each of us is unique and endowed with great
potential, but we exist in a kind of waking sleep because of our
early childhood programming. . . . In order to know ourselves and
evolve in positive ways, we first need to see that we essentially operate in a kind of 'waking sleep.' Without conscious effort, we function to a large degree mechanically, according to habitual patterns,
as we go about our everyday lives. Our 'sleep' is the unexamined
belief we all have that we live lives of relatively unlimited freedom,
when the opposite is true: We respond in predictable, repetitive
ways according to the dictates of our early programming."

Beatrice Chestnut, *The Complete Enneagram*[11]

Envision: A Time to Think

One important mental exercise in the Heartlift Method is heart-lifting—a cognitive reframing workout. Earlier, I shared one of my workouts; now, it is your turn.

Choose one trigger event that recently occurred in your life. Use the following chart for your mental workout. Refer to my earlier example if you need a jumpstart.

Date/Time	Trigger Event	Initial Emotional Response	Automatic Thought	Reframed Thought

Using an assessment tool from cognitive behavioral therapy (CBT), consider your highly personalized, automatic, go-to thought and ask yourself these questions:

- What is the evidence the automatic thought is true?
- What is the evidence the automatic thought is not true?
- What is the worst thing that can happen if it is true?
- What is the best thing that can happen if it is true?
- What is most likely to happen, based on the evidence?
- How is the automatic thought affecting how I act and feel?

- What would be the effect of changing my thought?
- What am I willing to do about it?[12]

Educate: A Time to Learn

Tool 3 is all about shaping a healthy thought life and getting to the bottom of unhealthy core beliefs, which include skewed perceptions. Self-awareness helps us improve our cognitive responses to seemingly insignificant misunderstandings. Sometimes we are just going to have a bad day or encounter someone else who is having a bad day. Other times, the silliest, most ordinary things will get under our skin and cause us distress. Our response is what I care about.

Our mental workout, heartlifting, helps us reframe unhealthy thought processes and reactions by increasing self-awareness. In keeping with our "out with the old, in with the new" theme, take a few minutes to reframe your old narrative. Here is mine again as an example:

My old narrative: Little Miss People Pleaser.

My old narrative's unhealthy thought: I want everyone to like me, and I'll do whatever it takes to make someone like me.

My new narrative: Woman Clothed in Strength and Dignity (Prov. 31:25).

My new narrative's healthy thought: I am clothed in God's strength and dignity and now accept, love, and value the God-breathed "me."

Now when you face a trigger event, head to the mental gym and work out these four exercises. In due time, with practice, this will become automatic.

My old narrative: _____

_____

_____

My old narrative's unhealthy thought: _____

_____

My new narrative: _____

_____

_____

My new narrative's healthy thought: _____

_____

Note: A fabulous personal growth tool for understanding the motives behind your thoughts and actions is found in the Enneagram, a system of nine personality types that offers profound insights into the way you think, feel, and behave.[13] I encourage you to take the time to take an Enneagram test, discover your "number,"[14] and learn about the motives behind your actions and thought processes. When studied and implemented, this emotional-health tool offers great wisdom, highly practical advice, and insightful ways to strengthen interpersonal relationships. One of my mentors, Beatrice Chestnut, writes, "As we begin to 'study' ourselves, it helps to have some sort of guidance. We think, feel, and do so many things every day—how can we even begin to make sense of it all? This is where the Enneagram comes in. As an ancient and universal model of human development and transformation, the Enneagram offers an accurate and objective view of the archetypal patterns that structure the human personality."[15]

Establish: A Time to Build

Think about this question: How do you know that the story you are telling yourself is actually your God-breathed story? Some experts call this "your essence" or "your true self." In our community, we refer to this as our God-breathed identity or story or self. As author and Enneagram teacher Ian Morgan Cron has taught me, "Sooner or later we must distinguish between what we are not and what we are. We must accept that fact that we are not what we would like to be. We must cast off our false, exterior self like the cheap and showy garment that it is. We must find our real self, in all its elemental poverty, but also in its great and very simple dignity: created to be the child of God, and capable of loving with something of God's own sincerity and his unselfishness."[16]

As we've already discovered, sometimes our stories are directed and narrated by the voices of others, by the voices of critics, by the voices of strangers, by the voices of unhealthy teachers/coaches/bosses, and so on. Some stories are passed down through generations. *We have a family business, and so you will work in that business. We are passionate and hot-headed. We are yellers and come from a long line of yellers.* Today, find your sacred space—your quiet place—and consider your answer to this question. I'll share my answer, then you share yours. Begin with "I know the story I am telling myself is true because . . ."

My answer: *I know the story I am telling myself is true because I've spent time thinking about and meditating on my Genesis 2:7 beginning.* *I've heard God-whispers that affirmed my*

God-breathed true self. I no longer abide by the old narrative, the old reels, the old tapes. I've overcome any and all negative narratives, labels, and words spoken by unhealthy voices in my life. I'm practicing how to discern the One True Voice (John 10:27). I'm aware of my unhealthy negative-feedback loop, and I am taking it off autopilot and rewiring my brain with a healthy positive-feedback loop. Today, I am speaking healing words, living into my new narrative, and committing to using the new emotional-health tools that will make me stronger every day.

Now it's your turn. How do you know that the story you are telling yourself is true?

_____

_____

_____

_____

_____

_____

PART TWO

Educate

EDUCATE (v) (Latin, *educo*, to lead out): To teach, train, or inform someone. Education, then, is to draw out or unfold the powers of the mind.

Open the eyes of their hearts, and let the light of Your truth flood in. Shine your light on the hope You are calling them to embrace. Reveal to them the glorious riches You are preparing as their inheritance.

Ephesians 1:18

TOOL 4

Shift from Shaming to Gracing
SELF-COMPASSION

THE INTENTION OF TOOL 4:
I shift from shaming language to grace language.

When we fight emotional pain, we get trapped in it. Difficult emotions become destructive and break down the mind, body, and spirit. Feelings get stuck—frozen in time—and we get stuck in them. The happiness we long for in relationships seems to elude us. We drag ourselves through the day, arguing with our physical aches and pains. Usually we're not aware just how many of these trials have their root in how we relate to the inevitable discomforts of life. Change comes naturally when we open ourselves to emotional pain with uncommon kindness. Instead of blaming, criticizing, and trying to fix ourselves (or someone else, or the whole world) when things go wrong and we feel bad, we can start with self-acceptance.

Christopher K. Germer, PhD, *The Mindful Path to Self-Compassion: Freeing Yourself from Destructive Thoughts and Emotions* can still smell the sterile atmosphere of my college medical center. A month into my senior year, I sat in a stark examination room, waiting to see the doctor on call. As I sat atop the cold stainless-steel table, my reflection gleamed in the polished paper towel holder on the wall. Surrounded by silence, I felt as if my reflection began to whisper, "How did you end up here? What a mess you've made." A multitude of disorganized thoughts whirled through my confused mind.

Imagine the headlines of the local paper: Miss Chesapeake—pregnant.

Imagine Mom: What on earth will this do to her?

Imagine the community: What about all the little girls who have looked up to me this year?

Imagine my future: So much for your dreams. You are such a failure.

For a brief moment, I felt like someone had turned the lights out on my life. Pleading my case before God, my heart desperately cried out, "Rescue me. Please, God, have mercy on me. Let the test be negative."

In sheer panic, my sincere Hail-Mary-pass plea continued, "God, please get me out of this mess. If you do, I promise to change my life and live for you." As the clock ticked in seeming slow motion, my pleas turned into profound silence. There were no words left, only fear and a very sober look into the current state of my life.

Finally, the door creaked open. In walked the stately doctor, in his starched white lab coat, shiny silver stethoscope carefully wrapped around his neck. Once again, I saw my reflection. Not a pretty sight. I looked up into his face—his strong features and piercing eyes looking back at me. They would be hard to forget. Reminding myself to breathe, my destiny felt as if it were standing on the edge of his next sentence.

"The test was negative, Miss Schoedler. You are not pregnant," he said sternly yet lovingly, much like a caring, concerned father might comfort his distressed daughter.

I heard four words: You. Are. Not. Pregnant.

Burying my head in my hands, relief swept over me. Time stood still, and I wept.

"Here, put these in your purse," he said, handing me a silver package. "Make sure you use them."

In his hand—a pack of birth control pills.

"Oh, no, Doctor," my weary voice cracked. "They won't be necessary."

"Go ahead, take them. You never know," he urged.

"No, believe me. Lesson learned."

On the long, frigid walk from the infirmary to my sorority house, the tears kept flowing. *If people knew the real me. My life is a facade, and I'm so tired of living it. I never wanted to have sex before marriage, and yet I did. What on earth was I thinking? Why did I give in? Why couldn't I say no?*

Loneliness and despair walked me home. As I entered my sorority house, utterly exhausted, my knees buckled. *Just make it to your room. Keep walking*, I thought. *That's it. One foot in front of the other.* By God's grace, I didn't see a single person I knew between the front door and my room.

Even my roommate was gone. Sacred space welcomed my hurting heart. A deep inner peace seemed to greet me as I stepped across the threshold of my door. As I locked the door behind me, everything familiar seemed to fade away. There, on my knees, I continued the conversation with God that had begun in the doctor's office.

Pregnant with the Wrong Dreams

Staying true to my word, right then and there, I surrendered to God. I wanted to live my life his way, not my way. Whispers of the Jesus I had heard about in Catholic Mass and Catholic school echoed in that room. "Faith words" spoken by friends in high school and college made their way from my head to my heart. It's hard to put the mystery of this giving your life to God into words, but it was, and still is, the best decision I have ever made.

That bleak, blustery October afternoon so long ago is still so fresh in my memory. To this day, the mystery of this spiritual transformation always takes my breath away. The essence of my old narrative reminds me of the loving care and deep concern of my heavenly Father—who is always ready and willing to help transform old negative narratives into beautiful new stories. Hindsight has taught me that regardless of the results of that pregnancy test—whether positive or negative—God knew the plans and purposes of my life (Jer. 29:11–14), and for some reason, a negative test result was the next step of my new narrative.

Even with a negative pregnancy test, though, I was indeed pregnant—pregnant with wrong plans and purposes, wrong dreams, and definitely the wrong person. In many ways, this entire ordeal served as a spiritual miscarriage. As painful and difficult as it all was, God my Father used the experience to help me find my way home to my true self, my essence. Somewhere, my true self had taken the wrong path and gotten very lost. She made many mistakes and forgot who she was born to be. But that moment in time was a divine invitation to pick up my brand-new pen and begin writing a brand-new story—the one God penned for me from the moment he breathed his breath of life into my being (Gen. 2:7).

The first chapter in my new story could have been titled "God Specializes in Tight Spots," and the first sentence could have read "God is a living, breathing reality and specializes in releasing fresh winds over a seeking heart." The words of Psalm 34:4–6 say it all:

> GOD met me more than halfway,
> he freed me from my anxious fears.
>
> Look at him; give him your warmest smile.
> Never hide your feelings from him.
>
> When I was desperate, I called out,
> and GOD got me out of a tight spot. (MSG)

The Shame Shutdown

I've rarely talked about this private part of my life—until now. As I've come to understand, timing is everything. I didn't have the necessary emotional tools to understand the ins and outs of that part of my story—until now. And, I'm here to help you understand your story—right now, in hopes that it will help you stay on the right path that leads you home to your true self.

For so many years, shame shut down the real me. In truth, the shame shutdown got a foothold in my life from an early age—six years old to be exact. On my sixth birthday, I had to stand on the white line of punishment during recess for talking too much in class (read more in *Overcoming Hurtful Words*[1]). My peers walked by, relishing my public scolding. I suppose my little-girl self decided right then and there that she didn't ever want to have that awful feeling—that is, shame—again. So I locked my true self, my fiery-redheaded, vivacious, outgoing, and passionate-about-life self, in a vault of fear and buried it deep under a front of futility. My false self hid behind the veneer of good works, the painful path of perfectionism, and a strong set of self-defeating survival mechanisms (see Tool 7).

I couldn't be myself because there was something essentially wrong with me. Or at least that is what I thought—cue cognitive distortion and unhealthy negative-feedback loops—and absorbed from standing on that white line.

In *The Soul of Shame*, Curt Thompson states, "Shame's presence is ubiquitous and inserts itself into the genetic material of the human storytelling endeavor."[2] He then encourages us

to envision shame as a personal attendant. Imagine that you have a completely devoted attendant attuned to every sensation, image, feeling, thought and behavior you have. However, imagine that your shame attendant's intention is not good, is not to care for you but rather to infuse nonverbal and verbal elements of judgment into every moment of your life. The word *attendant* at first may seem counterintuitive, as it usually applies to someone who has our best interest in mind. But this is how shame works, a wolf disguised in sheep's clothing. Hence, our shame attendant appears in language, feelings, sensations and images that may on the surface seem acceptable, common and normal, but its purpose is anything but helpful.[3]

My personal shame attendant pummeled my thought life, persistently whispering the following:

Good girls don't get pregnant out of wedlock.

Good girls follow the rules.

Good girls stifle their true voice and stand on the white line of fear and insecurity.

Good girls never make mistakes.

Good girls always do what is expected of them.

Good girls who do good deeds get into heaven.

(And perhaps the most damaging whisper of all) When and if you show your true self, nobody will love you. You will be all alone.

Maybe you have your own shame attendants. What damaging whispers have perpetually distorted your thought life and held you captive in a prison of self-defeating behaviors (2 Cor. 10:5)? As you read this chapter, make note of them. Declare a demolition day in which you tear down any and all "walls" or "old mental structures."

Demolish, from Latin root, *demoliri*, "tear down."[4]	Captive, from Latin root, *captivus*, "caught, taken prisoner."[5]
• To destroy the structural character of (a building, wall, etc.) by violently pulling it down.	• Made prisoner, enslaved.
• To destroy, tear down.	• To take, hold, seize, grasp.
• To lay waste.	• Taken and kept in confinement; completely in the power of another.
• To consume.	

Get to your good emotional bones. From this day forward, the "old" has no key and no access. Angels of God's love guard the door to your new God-breathed life.

A Special News Report on *The Guise of Shame*

We interrupt our regular programming—that is, chapter flow—to make this special announcement: shame is sneaky, underhanded, and highly toxic. Therapist and author Hilary McBride states, "Shame is a reduction of the essence of being alive. It tells us there is something wrong with who I am at my core."[6]

Look at the following dictionary meanings connected to this shady character, and you'll gain insight into the potential wreckage words of shame can cause:

- shame (n): "Painful feeling of humiliation or distress caused by the consciousness of wrong or foolish behavior."[7]

- humiliate (v): "Make (someone) feel ashamed and foolish by injuring their dignity and pride."[8]

- ashamed (adj): "Embarrassed or guilty because of one's actions, characteristics, or associations."[9]

- disgrace (n): "Loss of reputation or respect as the result of a dishonorable action."[10]

- sneaky (adj): "Furtive; sly."[11]

- underhanded (adj): "Acting or done in a secret or dishonest way."[12]

- subterfuge (n): "Deceit used in order to achieve one's goals."[13]

- furtive (adj): "Attempting to avoid notice or attention, typically because of guilt or a belief that discovery would lead to trouble."[14]

Notice the spiral of self-defeating, oppressive emotions. As you read through these words, does anyone come to mind? Who do you know that excels in deception; artful subterfuge; secretive, subtle, dishonest, and underhanded work?

Hint: he was ousted from heaven (Isa. 14), took the form of a serpent in the garden of Eden (Gen. 3), and became known as "the father of lies." Consider how John, one of Jesus's closest followers, describes this shame attendant: "You are of your father the devil, and it is your will to practice the desires [which are characteristic] of your father. He was a murderer from the beginning and does not stand in the truth because there is no truth in him. When he lies, he speaks what is natural to him, for he is a liar and the father of lies and half-truths" (John 8:44 AMP). See the emphasis on half-truths here. He's the father of *anything* untrue.

Have these clues helped you identify the author of such unhealthy behaviors?

Yes, you are wise indeed! Often known as Lucifer or Satan, in this book we will refer to him as Satan or perhaps give him a blunter nickname—Liar. I like calling him out for what he really is—a liar. Why? Because it is his sole mission to keep us locked in an emotional state of shaming lies, and he is very, very good at what he does. Author and host of Typology, Ian Cron, says this about shame:

> Love is the most powerful force in the universe, but it is neck and neck with shame. I think shame is an inch or two behind, actually, in terms of its influence on the human life. Shame is all about exposure—the fear of being revealed, found out, the flaws unveiled. Observe: How often is shame at the wheel of your car? Christianity and the grace it offers in the theology of grace can rewind the momentum of shame; it can also be weaponized and turned

into a force for creating shame. Shame is a "shadow government" running in our heads.[15]

How many adults have grown up hearing "Shame on you!" (with a finger pointing in their face), subconsciously absorbing and interpreting those words as highly personal: "You are bad, unworthy of anything good"? For children, who have only a few emotional-health tools and a not-yet-developed capacity for spiritual discernment, it can be quite difficult to separate shame from our personal identity or sense of self. We can know it is not right or acceptable or good but have no ability—no fully developed emotional or relational tools—to keep it from being subconsciously stored in our implicit memory.

"Shame on you!" means shame is being put on you, literally. The apostle Paul pleads with Christ's followers: "Do not let unwholesome [foul, profane, worthless, vulgar] words ever come out of your mouth, but only such speech as is good for building up others, according to the need and the occasion, so that it will be a blessing to those who hear [you speak]" (Eph. 4:29 AMP).

Words matter. We can't shortchange how much impact they have on our personal development and the course of our future.

Shame researcher Brené Brown shapes the severity of shame's stronghold in these most powerful words: "I define shame as the intensely painful feeling or experience of believing that we are flawed and therefore unworthy of love and belonging—something we've experienced, done, or failed to do makes us unworthy of connection. I don't believe shame is helpful or productive. In fact, I think shame is much more likely to be the source of destructive, hurtful behavior than the solution or cure. I think the fear of disconnection can make us dangerous."[16]

Learning a New Language

Love is God's language. And if love is God's language, might shame be the Liar's language? Dr. Curt Thompson affirms and adds, "This phenomenon [shame] is the primary tool that evil leverages, out of which emerges everything we would call sin. As such, it is actively, intentionally, at work both within and between individuals. Its goal is to disintegrate any and every system it targets, be that one's personal story, a family, marriage, friendship, church, school, community, business or political system. Its power lies in its subtlety and its silence, and it will not be satisfied until all hell breaks loose. Literally."[17]

In a self-absorbed society such as ours, lies are being told. It is painful to stand by and watch women, perhaps like you, believe these lies. Our stories may be different or quite similar. Tight spots take on a whole lot of sizes and shapes. One thing is certain. Shame, and all of its attendants, does everything in its power to keep you in a state of feeling reduced, humiliated, and devalued—and, most certainly, feeling unworthy of belonging and connection: first, from yourself, which involves a process called embodiment,[18] and second, from others, which involves emotional detachment.

This, my friend, is the most dangerous part of shame. It not only thrives in secrecy, silences our God-breathed voice, craves isolation, and fiercely oppresses the power of a healthy mind but also deprives us of true emotional and relational intimacy.

The Shame Shake-Off

Maybe you are hearing the shame-whisper of all whispers: *When and if you show your true self, nobody will love you. You will be all alone.*

Shame-whispers come, sometimes overtly, sometimes subtly, from

- an overbearing parent or unhealthy family system
- a narcissistic employer
- know-it-all peers
- authoritarian organizations or groups
- demeaning teachers or coaches
- playground bullies
- self-righteous men and women
- unrealistic cultural expectations and norms
- complete strangers

They speak unhealthy words that harm and hinder: *If you don't do this for me, I will fire you. You better give me your lunch, or I will beat you up. If you don't do it this way, don't come here anymore.*

Satan is the father of lies (John 8:44). Jesus is the truth (John 14:6). If I believe and adhere to the truth, how, then, do I slip into allowing shame to tell me I am bad?

I can't be bad when I have God's breath in me.

I can *do* bad, but I am not bad.

In Romans 3:23, Paul assures us that "all have sinned and fall short of the glory of God" (NIV). It is a spiritual truth that I have the propensity for "doing bad," but as a creation of God, I am not bad. There is a great difference between "doing" and "being."

Right here and right now, please repeat after me "The Shame Shake-Off Prayer":

There have been shame lies spoken over my heart, mind, and body.

Today, I believe the truth about myself.

I am lovable.

I am worthy of connection.

I make mistakes; I am not a mistake.

I fail; I am not a failure.

Even at my lowest, I have value, worth, and dignity.

Even in my tightest spots, I matter.

Even when I make a mess of things, I am seen, loved, and accepted by God.

From this day forward, I will do my best to tell the whole truth and nothing but the truth, so help me God. No hiding behind facades or pretense or excuses or denial.

I release the shame narrative and embrace the healing words of my heavenly Father, who breathed his breath into me.

From this moment on, I walk with my head held high.

From this moment on, I live forgiven, free, and full of faith.

From this moment on, I offer the gift of grace to myself and to others.

From this moment on, I speak healing words to myself and others.

From this moment on, I live into the meaningful new life God has for me.

Amen.

Grace Lifts the Weight of Shame

Perhaps the most difficult part of living into my beautiful new story when I was in college was telling my boyfriend, whom I thought I would marry, about my new relationship with God. Sometimes, letting go of the hand of our past is painfully hard. After all, a little bit of love is better than no love, right? A little bit of attention is better than no attention. Even though I knew our relationship was unhealthy and that I was selling myself short, I desperately feared being alone. Over Christmas break, we decided to meet and talk this through face-to-face. I did my best to share my transformative story in the hope that he might have a change of heart too.

"How can you leave me for a man you have never seen before?" he asked, honestly bewildered and very confused. "How do you know this man called Jesus is even real?" Through blinding tears, I tried to explain my newfound faith. We talked late into the night.

"Because I know. I can't explain it, but I know what I experienced was real. Now, my eyes are open, and I see that our relationship isn't healthy. We can't go on this way. I want to live for God, and you don't even believe in him."

"I'll never understand it," he said while shaking his head.

"I can't say that I do either. I just know I have to follow God's leading," I said. "Hopefully, one day, we will understand. At least I will pray for that."

Closing that door and saying goodbye felt much like a death. As I walked away from his car, my anguished heart collapsed into tears. The truth is, part of me needed to die.

My desperate need for love and security, at any cost, needed to die. My boyfriend's counterfeit love was better than no love, or so I thought. But in the depths of my heart, a little voice assured me: *He was not the right man for you. He was not part of God's plan and purpose for your future.* Now I see that his presence was keeping me from God's meaningful plan and purpose for my life (Eph. 1:18).

We must always be cautious. Sometimes our unhealthy sense of self gets in the way of our God-breathed capacity and purpose. That is why we must earnestly seek to live a wide-awake life and surround ourselves with emotionally healthy spaces, places, and faces. We won't do this perfectly, as none of us are perfect, but as those who are committed to practicing all things healthy. For a season, I accepted and allowed vain promises and hollow love into my life. These ultimately left me feeling empty, used, unfulfilled, and immensely lonely. My tireless quest for love was an exhausting and oftentimes debilitating exercise of overachieving, shame, empty affection, and mindless, futile nights of parties, senseless chatter, and wasted hours. A very unhealthy part of me needed to die.

At the time, I honestly didn't realize I was trying to fill a gigantic gaping hole in my heart—left by a father who was blinded by a bottle of alcohol. I was drowning in an emotional hangover, lost in insecure attachment, and these hurtful behaviors left my heart gasping for air. There seemed to be no way of escape. No way out. No other choice.

Until the arms of true freedom embraced my heart. As I surrendered the unhealthy parts of myself to God, an overwhelming sense of love surrounded me. *I felt strangely at peace.*

I began to actually feel a newfound sense of grace lifting the unbearable weight of shame from my shoulders. For the first time in my life, I felt grace do the following:

1. Offer a revolutionary truth: I didn't have to settle for less than best. Good isn't good enough for a great God. He

invites us to greatness by extending us his goodness (Rom. 2:4).

2. Pick me up off the floor, take my hand, and begin walking me into my future.

3. Help me understand that God was very real and extremely involved in helping me find the right path for not only my life but also the life of my legacy.

God's grace saved me, and for that, I am very grateful. Sleep came easily that night as 2 Corinthians 5:17 overtook my life: "Therefore, if anyone is in Christ, the new creation has come: The old has gone, the new is here!" (NIV). I wish I could say that I woke up the next day absolutely whole, but that would be a lie. A tremendous struggle ensued, for years, as I picked up my pen and started writing my new story. But I can assure you that grace was at my bedside each morning, helping me write every word of my God-breathed identity.

"Owning our story can be hard," writes Brené Brown, "but not nearly as difficult as spending our lives running from it. Embracing our vulnerability is risky, but not nearly as dangerous as giving up on love and belonging and joy—the experiences that make us most vulnerable. Only when we are brave enough to explore the darkness will we discover the infinite power of light."[19]

Grace Transforms Your Story

Today is no ordinary day. It is the day grace transforms your story. Shame can't exist when we embrace and speak healing words over every single area of our lives.

A long time ago, another woman found the amazing grace of Jesus. The Bible doesn't tell us much about her circumstances, only that the people in her town shunned and shamed her. We don't know her name. We don't know her family of origin or any of her history of hurts. We only know that she lived in a town in Samaria called Sychar (John 4:5), had five husbands, and was currently living with another man. We aren't told if her five husbands died or divorced her; all we know is she had five of them—giving the impression that she wasn't highly regarded by her community. We can read between the lines of her story and sense the shaming attendants at work. One hot afternoon, while doing an ordinary daily task, she had a life-changing encounter. At an ordinary well in her ordinary city, she met a seemingly ordinary man but who appeared to know everything about her.

I can't help but wonder. If she could tell us her story, what would she say? Taking a whole lot of creative license, let's pretend her journal has been discovered in an archeological dig of that area, and we are privy to her thoughts . We open to her entry, "The Day I Met the Man Called Jesus."

She begins:

It was a hot day. With each breath of the thick, humid air, it felt harder and harder to put one foot in front of the other. The taste of dust coated my tongue. Sweat dripped down my face like muddy tears. Today, even my bones ached. The chatter inside my head was as chaotic and confusing as my life. I couldn't help but wonder how my life had come to this. I thought, *Why am I more tired than usual? Is it because of the harsh words spoken to me yesterday? Are the years and years of aches, pains, and heartbreaks now forming one big ache?*

Finally, I saw Jacob's well, a sight for my very sore feet. It was not much farther. I kept telling myself, over and over again, *You can do this. Put one foot in front of the other.* It would have been so much easier in the early morning hours, but coming at noon saved me from the judging eyes of the other women. Maybe one day, but not today. I am so done with their glaring and staring. Don't they know I can hear their whispers?

I saw him sitting on the edge of the well—alone and seemingly content to be there. The bricks were cool, I supposed, a welcome relief from the heat of the day. I wanted to sit down, but that would have caused even more scandal. From the way he was dressed, I could tell he was a Jew—so not only a man but a Jewish man. I put my water pitcher down and placed my hand on my burning shoulder—rubbing it in hopes of easing the pain. More thoughts rolled through my mind. *When would somebody care about me? When would someone love me for me? When would I ever feel like I belong in this community?*

I was so tired. I'd had enough. I wanted to go to sleep. Yes, sleep, forever and ever and ever. *No one would miss me, that is for sure.*

Suddenly, he spoke, his dialect again pointing to his Jewish heritage. His voice was bold and strong—and oddly caring, like a concerned father might speak to a distressed daughter. He didn't speak to me like other men. His voice was different.

Very, very different.

Men in my city didn't talk to me, at least not with the kindness I heard in this man's voice. There was something unique about him. I couldn't quite put my finger on it, but suddenly I didn't feel like falling asleep. In truth, I felt wider awake than ever. His eyes were warm and welcoming, insightful, as if he looked straight through me and right into my soul.

At first, I felt very uncomfortable, but his words and his presence calmed me. Little did I know, at that very moment, how much my life was about to change.

A Jesus Encounter through the Eyes of John

The rich conversation between Jesus and the Samaritan woman is told to us through the eyes of the beloved disciple John—a man who had walked with Jesus and was "an eyewitness," as scholars call him, to Jesus's ministry here on earth. In John 4:7–42, he writes in detail of the strange and unusual encounter between Jesus and this woman. Let's pause and read through their conversation, line by line, up to the moment when Jesus reveals her history of hurts:

> **Jesus:** Would you draw water, and give Me a drink?
> **Woman:** I cannot believe that You, a Jew, would associate with me, a Samaritan woman; much less ask me to give You a drink. Jews, you see, have no dealings with Samaritans.
> **Jesus:** You don't know the gift of God or who is asking you for a drink of this water from Jacob's well. Because if you did, you would have asked Him for something greater; and He would have given you the living water.
> **Woman:** Sir, You sit by this deep well a thirsty man without a bucket in sight. Where does this living water come from? Are You claiming superiority to our father Jacob who labored long and hard to dig and maintain this well so that he could share clean water with his sons, grandchildren, and cattle?
> **Jesus:** Drink this water, and your thirst is quenched only for a moment. You must return to this well again and again. I offer water that will become a wellspring within you that gives life throughout eternity. You will never be thirsty again.

Woman: Please, Sir, give me some of this water, so I'll never be thirsty and never again have to make the trip to this well.
Jesus: Then bring your husband to Me.
Woman: I do not have a husband.
Jesus: Technically you are telling the truth. But you have had five husbands and are currently living with a man you are not married to. (John 4:8–18)

Meeting Jesus for the First Time

It doesn't matter how many times I read this story; it always gets to me. I connect so deeply to this woman's distress and feelings of loneliness. I empathize with her hidden struggle with shame. I sense we experienced the same quiet loneliness and deep longing to be seen and valued and worthy of real love. It seems she was settling for a little love being better than no love and perhaps didn't even know why she was doing so.

Something tells me she heard the same shame attendant: *When and if you show your true self, nobody will love you. You will be all alone.*

Just now, as I read this passage again, tears form in my eyes. I remember the words of famed late-eighteenth–early-nineteenth-century Bible scholar F. B. Meyer in his commentary on John 4 (KJV). He notes that Jesus had to evoke "the naked story of her past"[20] by saying, "Go, call thy husband!" With keen spiritual *and* psychological insights, he writes: "What a train of memory that word [husband] evoked! . . . But why awake such memories? Why open the cupboard-door and bid that skeleton down? . . . Why lay bare that life secret? It could not be otherwise. The wound must be probed to the bottom and cleansed, ere it could be healed. There must be confession before forgiveness. . . . This woman must judge her past sins in the light of those pure eyes, ere she could know the bliss of the fountain opened within the soul."[21]

This is the Jesus I met so long ago. A man with pure, piercing eyes who looked deeply through my eyes and into my aching, lost soul. A man who invited me to change. Yes, I had heard about Jesus growing up. Sunday after Sunday, I sat in the pew of my Catholic church. I attended catechism classes during my formative years and even considered (for a brief postcollege period) becoming a nun. So I knew "of" Jesus—that is, I had head knowledge—but it wasn't until I had my very own "ancient well" experience on that stainless-steel examination table that I actually "met" Jesus for the first time. *Head knowledge became a deep heart connection* (see the following illustration[22]).

Here, in this sacred intersection of head and heart, authentic faith—based on relationship, not an established religious system—is born. This is where the heartshift* happens, and nothing is ever the same again. Respected theologian Philip Yancey, author of *The Jesus I Never Knew*, writes, "Jesus invoked a different kind of power: love, not coercion. No one who meets Jesus ever stays the same."[23]

Author and Bible scholar John Kohlenberger III adds to this understanding of Jesus. He writes, "In a culture characterized by social status and power, Jesus ushered in a brand-new definition of authority, and his acceptance of women was nothing short of radical. . . . Interestingly, every woman that Jesus encountered in the Gospels—no matter her ethnicity or socioeconomic class—was raised in her spiritual and physical state as well as in her social status."[24]

Perhaps your God narrative—your perception or thoughts or first encounters with Jesus—has been blurred, broken, bruised, or even forced on you in a religious manner with strict rules, restrictions, regulations, and rituals. *Do this. Don't do that.*

Maybe you've been in a religious system that doesn't share Jesus's radical acceptance of women.

I completely understand.

But today I ask you to take a few minutes out of your day to pause and reflect on what we've talked about up to this point. Don't let the words *sin, confession,* or *repentance* scare you. They are theological terms we don't hear as often anymore. Simply put, they are invitations to face "the naked story of our past" and, in doing so, to ask God for forgiveness in order to move forward into our new, God-breathed story. Pastor and author of *The Message*, Eugene Peterson reminds us that repentance means "a man should reverse directions, change the mode of life to which he had become accustomed, and reorient himself."[25] He states clearly that repentance is "not a word of feeling at all, but a word of action. . . . You repent only when you turn around and go back or toward God."[26]

Allow some space in your life to talk with Jesus, to lay bare the naked story of your past. He is waiting for you because he loves you deeply.

A Jesus Encounter

After writing these words, I needed a break. Laying bare the naked stories of our pasts is deep, often draining, work. I've learned the hard way to implement self-care, so I went out for a walk. Within minutes, I came upon an old wooden bench under the covering of an old tree. It looked out over a small lake. I paused and thought of sitting down and having a quiet moment, but it was cold and misting, and the sun was setting.

I best be about my walk, I thought. *Keep going.*

But when I passed it on my return, I felt compelled to sit down. I sat on the bench and listened for God-whispers.

Something special happened when I stopped walking and sat down. When I stop moving and doing and make space for being, I tend to hear God's voice—and it usually comes in a whisper. Not an audible one, but something I sense in my soul.

Stillness creates an atmosphere for God-whispers. Maybe that is why it is so hard to be still. The Liar knows the power of this sacred space, so he works very hard to keep us moving and doing. In his national bestseller, *2 Chairs: The Secret that Changes Everything*, author Bob Beaudine shares a life lesson he learned from his mother. She told him, "There is nothing that you could do or think of in life that would be more important than setting this up right now and doing it."[27]

Setting what up? I thought, as I was reading the book.

Let me simplify her advice. Set up two chairs: one for you, one for God. (Or maybe, like me, you find a bench.) Grab a cup of coffee or tea and sit down with him. Talk to him like you'd talk to a friend.

Sounds simplistic, doesn't it? A little too easy or sacrilegious? Aren't we supposed to be all pious when we talk to God?

Jesus left us with these very special words: "I don't call you servants any longer; servants don't know what the master is doing, but I have told you everything the Father has said to Me. I call you friends" (John 15:15).

This is the Jesus I know and love. Sometimes we will sit on a stainless-steel examination-room table. Sometimes we will sit by an ancient well. Sometimes we will sit on an old park bench under the canopy of a winter tree.

And there, in our stillness, we will hear God-whispers.

Here is what I heard today as I sat on that old wooden bench: *Janell, shame is no longer writing your story. Grace picked up the pen a long time ago, but you didn't give it full rein. Today is that day. I want you to begin fully living your beautiful new story. I want you to receive the same living water I offered the Samaritan woman. It is yours.*

Today, dear friend, we pick up our pens.

Today, we begin letting grace write our story.

Today, we turn fully toward God and receive his living water.

Stay tuned. There is a brilliant finish to our Samaritan woman's story. We'll talk more about her as we move through the nine tools. Until then, hear grace's whisper of all whispers: When you show your true self, I will be with you. I will guide you to a healthy, loving community who values your humanity and journeys with you toward emotional health and wellness. From this moment on, you are clothed in strength and dignity, and you can definitely smile at your future (Prov. 31:25).

Strength Training for the Soul

Today's Heartlift: "Of course, adult life is not always so simple. Some issues need to be revisited—not dropped—and talk is essential to this process. We need words to begin to heal betrayals, inequalities, and ruptured connections.

Our need for language, conversation, and definition goes beyond the wish to put things right. Through words we come to know the other person—and to be known. This *knowing* is at the heart of our deepest longings for intimacy and connection with others. How relationships unfold with the most important people in our lives depends on courage and clarity in finding voice. This is equally true for our relationship with our self."

Harriet Lerner, *The Dance of Connection*[28]

Envision: A Time to Think

The fatigue of living in the guise of shame catches up with us. Today, grace invites us to open our closet (or our cupboard) and let the skeletons out—one story at a time. In fact, why not gut our closets to their emotional bones and design a whole new closet? Shame deceives us into thinking it is easier to deny the facts than to face them. Shame's plan is to rob us of our God-breathed destiny. But that plan, my friend, is about to be foiled. Let grace help you live into the beautiful new life God has planned for you since the moment he breathed his breath into you. (Read more about this in my book *Overcoming Hurtful Words*, practice 3).

Grab your Bible and turn once again to our story in John 4:1–42. In *lectio divina* tradition, read this passage as if you are the Samaritan woman who meets Jesus at an ancient well. See a circumstance, conversation, or chaotic period in your life through the eyes of this caring, concerned man called Jesus and through the lens of grace. Sit in a chair or on a bench and listen for God-whispers; you'll be so glad you did.

Before moving on, let's make sure we fully understand the clear distinction between guilt and shame. In "Why Shame and Guilt Are Functional for Mental Health," author and psychologist Joaquín Selva writes, "Someone who feels guilty regrets some behavior they exhibited, while someone who feels shame regrets some aspect of who they are as a person. This is sometimes called the 'self-behavior distinction.' . . . Following this logic, it is much easier to alleviate feelings of guilt than shame, as making up for bad behavior is easier than fundamentally changing oneself."[29] In the simplest of terms, "Shame says, 'I am bad.' Guilt says, 'I did something bad.'"[30]

Educate: A Time to Learn

In my own *lectio divina* with John 4:1–42, I found myself mesmerized by the dialogue between Jesus and this woman. I realized how much I identified with the woman at the well, particularly her avoidance of meeting with the other women of the city and her isolation from them. Women typically drew water in the cool of the evening. But the woman we meet here with Jesus came to the well at noon, in the heat of the day, which hints at her sense of shame and unworthiness. Recall Curt Thompson's piercing description of "a shame attendant": "Envision shame as a personal attendant . . . a completely devoted attendant attuned to every sensation, image, feeling, thought and behavior you have. . . . Her intention is not good, is not to care for you but rather to infuse nonverbal and verbal elements of judgment into every moment of your life."[31]

My personal shame attendant kept me from returning to my university alma mater for thirty years. *You did some shameful things, Janell. You are a really bad person. No one will accept that you've changed. Don't ever go back; you'll be sorry you did.*

Let's return to our earlier question. Maybe you have your own shame attendants. What damaging whispers have pummeled your thought life and stalled your movement forward? Reconcile them now. In a quiet place, bring your history of hurts into the present to make meaning and sense of them. Forgive yourself. Receive God's forgiveness. *Live in your newfound freedom.*

Establish: A Time to Build

Using the following chart, meditate on 2 Corinthians 12:9: "My grace is sufficient for you [My lovingkindness and My mercy are more than enough—always available—regardless of the situation]; for [My] power is being perfected [and is completed and shows itself most effectively] in [your] weakness" (AMP).

When Grace Writes Your Story	When Shame Writes Your Story
Grace defined: "Of the merciful kindness by which God, exerting his holy influence upon souls, turns them to Christ, keeps, strengthens, increases them in Christian faith, knowledge, affection, and kindles them to the exercise of the Christian virtues."[32]	Shame defined: "The intensely painful feeling or experience of believing that we are flawed and therefore unworthy of love and belonging—something we've experienced, done, or failed to do makes us unworthy of connection."[33]

continued

131

When Grace Writes Your Story	When Shame Writes Your Story
Grace = Jesus's death on the cross redeemed every single "bad thing" I have done and will ever do (John 1:10–18). Grace speaks the language of self-compassion. Author Kristin Neff writes, "Instead of mercilessly judging and criticizing yourself for various inadequacies or shortcomings," offer yourself "kind[ness] and understanding when confronted with personal failing—after all, who ever said you were supposed to be perfect?"[34]	Shame = "I am bad." Shame wants to hide, isolate, and escape. Guilt = "I did something bad." Guilt wants to repent, forgive, and repair. Guilt is a God-given sense that "sin"—a fault, a besetting unhealthy pattern or behavior, a lapse of judgment, and so on—needs to be attended to. It leads us to transformation. The psalmist David beautifully guides the practice of confession and repentance in Psalm 51:1–12.
God-whispers share liberating truth and are covered in love: *You made a mistake. Ask God for forgiveness. Forgive yourself. Learn from this and move forward. Next time, you'll do better because you know better.*	Shame attendants speak oppressive lies that are covered in judgment: *You are such a mistake. You always mess up, don't you? When will you get it together? Truth is, you will never learn. Give up.*
Speak this heartlifting Scripture every single morning: "My grace is sufficient for you [My lovingkindness and My mercy are more than enough—always available—regardless of the situation]; for [My] power is being perfected [and is completed and shows itself most effectively] in [your] weakness" (2 Cor. 12:9 AMP).	Speak these healing words over your day; make it personal: "[Insert your name], be prepared. You're up against far more than you can handle on your own. . . . [Use] every weapon God has issued. . . . Truth, righteousness, peace, faith, and salvation are more than words. Learn how to apply them. You'll need them throughout your life" (Eph. 6:13–14 MSG).

TOOL 5

Speak Healing Words to Your Future

HEALTHY ASSERTIVENESS

THE INTENTION OF TOOL 5:
I speak healing words to my future.

The people we surround ourselves with either raise or lower our standards. They either help us to become the best version of ourselves or encourage us to become lesser versions of ourselves. We become like our friends. No man becomes great on his own. No woman becomes great on her own. The people around them help to make them great. We all need people in our lives who raise our standards, remind us of our essential purpose, and challenge us to become the best version of ourselves.

Matthew Kelly, *The Rhythm of Life: Living Every Day with Passion and Purpose*

H i, Janell," I heard a sweet voice say on the other end of the phone. "I have something exciting to ask you."

"Well, hello, Renee," I said. "It is so good to hear your voice. It's been a while. How is college going for you?"

Renee and I attended the same home church. During her high school years, we had many interesting conversations about faith and ministry. At the time, I was traveling, speaking, and mentoring younger women. Renee, a vivacious rising leader, aspired to develop her own speaking and teaching gifts and often asked me questions about the process.

Her call was a welcome surprise.

"What are you doing the first weekend in February?" she asked. "The women of InterVarsity would love to have you come speak to us at our first women's conference. I know you have a busy speaking schedule, but it would be so awesome to have you as our keynote speaker, especially since you are an alumni and InterVarsity was such an important part of your college experience. What do you think? Do you think that might be possible?"

"Wow. What a surprise," I gasped. "Really? This is astounding. Never in a million years did I expect this invitation, so let me catch my breath and I'll give you a call in a few days."

I hadn't been back to my college campus since the day I graduated—almost thirty years earlier. Isn't it amazing how long a shadow shame can cast? I'd been to the city, visited friends, and taken my son to soccer tournaments at a nearby college, but I hadn't returned to campus. *Too many haunting memories.* Much like the woman at the well, I now understand that I avoided my past and kept it locked away in a closet of shame skeletons.

If people see the real me, they won't like me.

I didn't say yes, at first. This request required some serious soul-searching and a whole lot of thought and prayer. On the one hand, standing in front of hundreds of collegiate women thrilled me. Returning to InterVarsity, the spiritual soil that nurtured and taught me so much about having a real relationship with Jesus, would be deeply rewarding. Being invited to speak absolutely humbled me.

On the other hand, baring my soul in front of hundreds of collegiate women scared me to death.

Tell my story? Be vulnerable? Unlock a closet of sleeping skeletons? Let people see the real me? Tell the whole truth and nothing but the truth, so help me God? Really not sure I'm up for that kind of transparency challenge.

Sometimes sharing our story is both riveting and really scary.

Days passed. I couldn't think of anything else. My husband and I prayed. I talked to my closest confidants. I even scheduled a session with my counselor. And, most importantly, I sat quietly before God. Then I felt a little nudge and heard two words, "Why not?" and two more questions: "What did I have to lose? *Nothing.* What did I have to gain? *Everything.*"

Greater than any fear I felt quaking inside my soul, I desperately wanted to share my story in hopes that it would help young women find the true freedom in Christ I had found so long ago.

Finally, I picked up the phone. I took a very big, very deep breath and whispered a brave, albeit very nervous, yes.

"Renee," I said, "I'll come. Let's do this."

A Walk of Shame Becomes a Walk of Grace

Before I could speak one word to those young women, I needed to do something else first: transform my *walk of shame* into a *walk of grace* (see Tool 4). Earlier in the day, I made my way to the Student Health Center, where shame had gotten ahold of me. I sat in my car for several minutes, trying to quiet my anxious, racing heart. *Why, after three decades, does this still make my entire body shake?* I thought.[1]

All I could do was pray my brave three-word prayer, *Help me, God.*

Finally, I made my way out of the car. *You've got this, girl. One foot in front of the other.*

There, outside the front door, was a bench. I felt it calling my name. I sat down, called my husband, and together we prayed the following:

- A prayer of gratitude for all God had done in our lives.
- A prayer covered in tears with one final whisper: "God, thank you that you are a turn-it-around God" (Gen. 50:20).
- "Today, I close the book written by shame" (Ps. 103:12).[2]
- "I begin living my God-breathed purpose" (2 Cor. 5:17).[3]

Bravely, I retraced my steps from the Student Health Center to my sorority house. I began to see this journey in an entirely different way. I began seeing it through my heavenly Father's eyes.

When I reached the sorority house, I was amazed. A bench was outside the front door. I didn't remember a bench being there, but it had been almost thirty years. God, in his loving, tender way, had a bench waiting just for me. I started to see a theme unfolding. Sometimes, altars take the form of very ordinary objects—in my case, these two simple benches became a holy place to pause for a few minutes and let my ancient heartrift experience a much-needed heartshift.

Surrender the Sting of Shame to the Shelter of Grace

This time, instead of calling my husband, I prayed the following alone:

- A prayer of gratitude for all God had done in my life.
- A prayer covered in peace with one final whisper: "God, today, I surrender the sting of shame to the shelter of grace."
- "Today, I let grace write my story" (Gal. 4:6).
- "Every single word I speak and live will be full of grace. Thank you."

I sat for a spell and savored the sunshine that filled that sacred space. Then I got up, took another deep, cleansing breath, and moved forward into my vision of victory.

That night, before opening my mouth, I took it all in. I feasted on the faces of an auditorium filled with young collegiate women, waiting to hear my story. With a deep sense of gratitude and an entirely new understanding of God's grace, I shared my story, and together we looked at the life of the Samaritan woman (John 4). Over the course of the weekend, we met several times, and each time I felt my heart open wider and wider.

I found myself speaking with a new voice—much like I imagine the Samaritan woman did—filled with a fresh understanding of my God-breathed value, worth, and dignity. Even though centuries separated us, both the Samaritan woman and I experienced the silencing of years of shame by the glorious gift of God's grace. Strange as it might sound, I felt like she held my hand and led me from a life of shame into a life of grace. Her freedom led her to her community in Sychar; my freedom led me to my alma mater.

Much to my amazement and sincere joy, the words of my story flowed like living water. *I bared my soul. I was vulnerable. I let the skeletons out, one by one. I accepted the transparency challenge.* And then, after all that, I watched a line begin to form of young women who desired to receive prayer and share their hearts with me. *Totally unbelievable.*

Some waited a very long time. The ordinary carpet of the ordinary conference room floor took the metaphorical form of an ancient well. We sat on the floor and talked for hours. One by one they awakened to shame's shrewd, subtle tactics and learned to shelter in the gracious presence of God's love. I looked through their eyes and into their souls and felt so deeply and profoundly connected. *What an honor*, I thought. *What a privilege to stand with them at this spiritual intersection in their lives.* The essence of pain became the fragrance of freedom.

The Power of Sharing our Stories

A couple of days later, I was sitting at my kitchen table grading papers when my phone rang. I was teaching middle and high school writing at the time, and I remember it as if it were yesterday. The time was 4:45 p.m. Dinner was bubbling on the stove. My body was weary from an extremely gratifying, yet very tiring weekend of speaking and connecting to these precious young women, standing on the threshold of the rest of their lives.

"Janell," the voice whispered. "I'm Heather, and I heard you speak this past weekend at JMU. I couldn't believe your story. It is now my story. I am living your story right now, and I am so scared. I don't know what to do. I hope you don't mind that I called, but I didn't know where else to turn. Thank you for giving us your number."

I could hear her crying and knew this phone call required a great deal of courage. I heard her say four words: "I think I'm pregnant."

"Okay," I said, her words an echo from my past. "Take a deep breath and tell me more. I'm here for you."

I then took my own deep breath—quickly assuming a listening-between-the-lines posture. I closed my computer, took my glasses off, and closed my eyes, silently praying for the right words to speak to this heart.

"Go ahead," I said. "I'm listening."

She shared her story. She was on edge because the young man, who she believed was the father, was on his way over to be with her as she took the pregnancy test. "It was only one time. I can't even believe I let this happen to me. What is wrong with me? I am so stupid. I know better.

"Oh," she said, "he's here. Please pray for me."

I prayed and told her to call me back as soon as she had taken the test.

About an hour passed and she called. The test was negative.

We talked for a while longer.

"Remember the woman we talked about this past weekend?" I asked. "The woman from Samaria, who met Jesus at the well? He offered her a new way of living her life. Now he offers you the same," I said. "It seems 'negative' is now part of your new narrative, as it was in my life so long ago. Take some time. I know how overwhelmed you must feel. Breathe deeply. I believe there will be a time for you to share your story, Heather, and I can't wait to hear how it unfolds."

"And Heather," I added, "please remember you have value, worth, and dignity. Maybe, like me, you've had the wrong plans and purposes, the wrong dreams, and even the wrong mindset. Culture has a strong voice, and sometimes without even knowing it, we believe that voice. It takes courage to swim against the tide. Take time to reflect deeply on what just unfolded and sit at the ancient well. Allow Jesus to speak to you, and I believe in time you will see your future through his eyes."

I hung up the phone in awe of God's compassion and love. We don't always get a second chance to revisit the regrets of our past. Poet and author David Whyte expresses this beautifully in his essay "Regret." "Regret is a short, evocative and achingly beautiful word; an elegy to lost possibilities. To admit regret is to understand we are fallible, that there are powers in the world beyond us. . . . Fully experienced, regret turns our eyes, attentive and alert, to a future possibly lived better than our past."[4]

I hope that my fully experienced regrets alerted Heather "to a future possibly lived better than our past."

Gobsmacked at God's Remarkable Timing

While I was in the midst of writing this chapter, my phone rang. This time it was my dear friend Sheryl, checking up on me.

"How's the writing going?" she asked.

"Good. A little different than I anticipated," I said. "I didn't expect to dig so deep into the realm of shame. It's so good, though, and it has been helpful to process it all. Having done so much work and study, there are new understandings and even deeper revelations unfolding—especially concerning the walk of shame to the walk of grace that I encountered a few years ago."

"Oh!" she said, as if she was sitting on the edge of her seat. "I have something I want you to watch, but you must promise me you won't read anything into it. It is just so powerful. You have to see it."

A few minutes later, she texted me a link to a YouTube video.

"Let me know what you think," she said. "I'll be waiting."

One minute and forty-seven seconds later, I found myself in an emotional heap.

Only one word describes that moment: gobsmacked. Our British friends use it when they are utterly astounded at something. The link took me to an excerpt from the season five finale of the popular *Game of Thrones* television show. One of the lead characters, Cersei Lannister, is forced to take the punishing penance of a walk of shame. The reenactment of this ancient medieval practice of shaming is graphic and disturbing, and it clearly tells the story.

The most alarming, or revealing, aspect of this scene is the woman following Cersei. With a big bell in her hand, she harshly, and with evil intent dripping from her lips, repeatedly says one word. After rewinding it several times, I homed in on exactly *what* she was saying.

I gasped.

Over and over again, she repeats, "Shame. Shame. Shame."

I immediately called Sheryl.

"Do you hear what she is saying?" I screamed, unable to contain my passion. "Unbelievable," I continued. "That is exactly how it feels when shame is on your back. And—that bell! Are you kidding me? It is an exact replica of the old bell used by my Catholic nuns."

A Jesus Encounter Changes Everything

Oh, friend, embrace this truth. We no longer have a shame attendant following us. The haunting sound of shame's handbell is hushed by the sweet song of God's amazing grace. Author Marcus Borg writes:

> The gospel of Jesus—the good news of Jesus' own message—is that there is a way of being that moves beyond both secular and religious conventional wisdom. The path of transformation of which Jesus spoke leads from a life of requirements and measuring up (whether to culture or to God) to a life of relationship with God. It leads from a life of anxiety to a life of peace and trust. It leads from the bondage of self-preoccupation to the freedom of self-forgetfulness. It leads from life centered in culture to a life centered in God.[5]

When we left the Samaritan woman in Tool 4, she had experienced a shocking, life-changing encounter with Jesus. She had gone to the well in her city to draw water and instead this man, Jesus, offered something called living water. There, by an ordinary well, Jesus revealed his personal insights and knowledge about her history of hurts and called her to live in a different way. Let's pick up her story where we left off.

A Jesus Encounter Empowers

In *Callings: Finding and Following an Authentic Life*, author Gregg Levoy writes, "Saying yes to the call tends to place you on a path that half of yourself thinks doesn't make a bit of sense, but the other half knows your life won't make sense without. This latter part, continually pushing out from within us with a centrifugal force, keeps driving us toward authenticity, against the tyranny of fear and inertia and occasionally reason, against terrific odds, and against the knocking in our hearts that signals the hour."[6] Sometimes, as in the life of the Samaritan woman, the call of Jesus won't make any sense at all. But deep down, she knew his words were truth and that she had to follow him. She came to Jacob's well to draw a pitcher of water; instead, she met a man who offered her living water, from which she

- drew a newfound sense of self
- returned and reclaimed the true essence of her Genesis 2:7 beginning
- "put off" her old narrative and "put on" her new narrative
- released the burdensome history of hurts and discovered the freedom of authentic faith
- embraced healing words and lived from a place of value, worth, and dignity
- most importantly, found her authentic voice and used it to advance the kingdom of God

The moment she realized that Jesus was the coming Messiah she'd heard so much about, she was empowered with a God-breathed capacity and purpose (John 4:25–26). This is what I love so much about Jesus. He looked deeper than her exterior and into the interior of her heart. *She didn't know what she needed to heal, but Jesus did.* We don't know the hard knocks or bad choices or series of unfortunate events that she met along her path. The beauty of Jesus is that he doesn't seem to care about any of that. He meets her right where she is—bad choices and big mistakes— and shows her another way.

I can't help but wonder if, when she returned to her community in Sychar, she, too, transformed her walk of shame into a walk of grace. The dusty path was now a path filled with light and love. Was there a skip in her step? Did she stop and consider all God had done for her? Upon her return, she tells them all, "I met a stranger who knew everything about me. Come and see for yourselves; can He be the Anointed One?" (John 4:29). We can only imagine their reaction. Did she look different? Was her countenance filled with "psychological brightness"[7] and joy? Did the living water of God's spirit flow out of her and drench the parched soul of the entire community too?

Many followed her back to the ancient well to see the stranger whose healing words transformed the community outcast into a new woman. John writes:

> Because one woman shared with her neighbors how Jesus exposed her past and present [can we add, "heartlifted" her], the village of Sychar was transformed—many Samaritans heard and believed. The Samaritans approached Jesus and repeatedly invited Him to stay with them, so He lingered there for two days on their account. With the words that came from His mouth, there were many more believing Samaritans. They began their faith journey because of the testimony of the woman beside the well; but when they heard for themselves, they were convinced the One they were hearing was and is God's Anointed, the Liberating King, sent to rescue the entire world. (John 4:39–42)

A Jesus Encounter Brings Healthy Assertiveness

Today, we would say the Samaritan woman "found her voice" and, as a result, began living into her beautiful new story. Scholars and theologians refer to her as "the first evangelist": "By the spirit, the woman acknowledged the truth of Christ's Messiahship and Omniscience and immediately became a powerful witness to her remarkable discovery. . . . Her mind grasped the secret of true worship and of Christ's mission, and her instinct for telling news became apparent as with the passion of an evangelist."[8] She couldn't keep her story to herself. It was far too good and had to be shared. As a result, we see her community transformed.

I equate "voice" with "value," and when we understand our value, we can't help but share our stories. They are far too good. We know that experiencing the power of a heartlift brings a strong sense of self, which brings healthy assertiveness—a core communication skill—and enables each of us to develop stronger relationships and stronger communities. According to the Mayo Clinic, healthy assertiveness does the following:

- Helps control stress and anger and improves coping skills.
- Helps effective self-expression and enables us to stand up for our points of view, while respecting the rights and beliefs of others.
- Fosters mutual respect, enabling diplomacy and integrity.
- Creates innate awareness of the rights of others, offering keen insights on resolving conflict.
- Makes communication direct and respectful and helps make the delivery of our messages—that is, our words and the tone of our voices—well received and ultimately successful.
- Directs the practice of emotion regulation—not too passive, not too aggressive, just right.[9]

Five Keys to Finding Your New Voice

When I began my own journey, I needed a great deal of help to understand what healthy assertiveness looked like in real life. I may have looked assertive on the outside, but I often found myself feeling timid and afraid to say what I wanted or needed to say, even within my own family. Little Miss People Pleaser became Little Miss Husband Pleaser, Little Miss Children Pleaser, and even Little Miss Church Lady Pleaser.

I didn't want to be rejected or misunderstood or left out.

I wanted everyone to be happy, even at the cost of my own emotional health.

Sometimes writing a new narrative is daunting. You may ask yourself, *Am I up to this? Does it even matter? Is what I am doing making any difference at all?* The answers: yes, yes, yes. Much like entering a new country, a new narrative requires learning a new language—the language of emotional, relational, and many times spiritual health.

The tools in this book work. They will work for you and help you find your voice. To increase your capacity for healthy assertiveness, which will improve everything in your life, adopt the following five keys to finding your VOICE to help you make the necessary changes to move forward:

1. *Value yourself and validate others.* Ask, *How do I talk to myself? Is my self-talk healthy or unhealthy?* Use your voice to speak healing words, first and foremost, to your own heart. Like the Proverbs 31 woman, clothe yourself and everyone in your sphere of influence with strength and dignity (v. 25). Live the Golden Rule and treat others as you would want to be treated (Matt. 7:12). Validating

others doesn't mean accepting any behavior, belief system, or bad choice. It does mean offering unconditional love, personal accountability, integrity, honesty, and above all else, mutual respect and trust. We can agree to disagree and still sit at the same table.

2. *Optimize your skills.* Invest time and energy into your mental health and personal development. Einstein is thought to have said, "Insanity is doing the same thing over and over again, expecting different results." If you want to become an effective communicator and enhance every relationship in your life, it will take an investment of time, energy, and sometimes money. If you don't know where to start, ask for help.[10] Always remember, asking for help is a sign of strength.

3. *Initiate healthy behavior patterns and healthy communication skills.* When a heartlifter—that is, a person committed to emotional health and wellness—is at the center of a family, community, workplace, or church, healthy relationships flourish. Be the one in the room to direct conversations that are healthy, diplomatic, and steeped in wisdom and integrity. There must be at least one person, one visionary, committed to seeing this change through to the end. Leaving a God-sized legacy is a God-sized task.

4. *Communicate clearly.* Be direct, diplomatic, and discerning. Say what you need to say with grace and candor. Instead of being a peacekeeper, become a peacemaker.[11] That might look like creating a bit of drama or tension or hard truth, but the result will be healthier relationships. Speak the truth in love and cover it with unconditional love. Instead of comparing, gossiping, berating, belittling,

or overpowering, use your voice to increase the value, worth, and dignity of others and to create a healthy atmosphere in the room or space where healing conversations take place—especially hard conversations. No finger-pointing, blaming, or shaming, and if at all possible, bring strength, not sarcasm.

5. *Energize the room.* Nothing sucks the life out of a room like unhealthy communication. *C* and *E* go hand in hand. As we develop the skill of communicating clearly, we will energize the room. Proverbs 14:1 serves as a great watchword: "The wise woman builds her house [on a foundation of godly precepts, and her household thrives], But the foolish one [who lacks spiritual insight] tears it down with her own hands [by ignoring godly principles]" (AMP).

Speak Healing Words

The human voice is a powerful instrument. Author and broadcaster Steve Henn writes, "A human voice still establishes a connection like nothing else can. A human voice can heal a country. Simply listening to someone tell their story can fill you with empathy and compassion. It can lead to forgiveness. Think of everything you learn by listening carefully to someone talk. Often you can guess their age and their gender. Maybe where they grew up. Often you can feel the emotions they feel—their happiness, their fear, their love."[12]

Imagine what it must have been like to be the Samaritan woman, sitting at that ancient well. Jesus's voice changed her and her community forever. It must have been warm and welcoming. It must have been gentle and kind. It must have been strong and trustworthy. He made her feel safe and secure and spoke words that looked through her eyes and into her soul. We have that same power and potential within our grasp. Will we use it wisely? Will we speak healing words? The choice is completely ours.

Strength Training for the Soul

Today's Heartlift: "Because assertiveness is based on mutual respect, it's an effective and diplomatic communication style. Being assertive shows that you respect yourself because you're willing to stand up for your interests and express your thoughts and feelings. It also demonstrates that you're aware of the rights of others and are willing to work on resolving conflicts."

Mayo Clinic[13]

Envision: A Time to Think

There is a fine line between assertiveness and aggression. Assertiveness is "being forthright about your own wants and needs, while still considering the rights, needs, and wants of others."[14] Assertive people are self-assured, confident, and empathic. Aggression is "do[ing] what is in your own best interest without regard for the rights, needs, feelings, or desires of other people."[15] Aggressive people are selfish, self-gratifying, and egocentric. While practicing assertiveness, keep these key points close in mind:

- Am I stating my point of view or request directly, diplomatically, and clearly?
- Am I practicing discretion and awareness of timing? Is this the right time? The right place?
- Am I speaking from a calm, centered place?

- Do I need to take a deep breath and find a few minutes to get to a calm, centered place?
- Am I listening between the lines so that I actually hear what is being said?
- Are my nonverbal cues (eye contact, tone of voice, facial expressions, body language) as direct, diplomatic, and clear as my words?
- Am I exaggerating, being overly dramatic, or making universal statements with words such as *always* and *never*?
- Am I speaking with facts, not judgments or supposition?
- Am I using *I* instead of *you*, so I don't enter the blaming and shaming game? Am I saying, "I feel this . . ." instead of "You make me feel . . ."?
- Am I collecting strength[16]—that is, practicing self-care and restoration daily, when and if I can, to make sure I am fully present to the other person? Do I need to examine my busyness?
- Am I making everybody's business my business and my business everybody's business? Or am I using discretion and being led by wisdom?

Educate: A Time to Learn

When I was a middle and high school writing teacher, I'd give my students a creative-writing prompt, set the timer for fifteen minutes, and let my students go. No concerns over punctuation or grammar, just writing from the heart. No grade assigned, just writing for pure expression. What happened in that short time was always so amazing. Today, let's take a few moments with the following creative-writing prompt. Set your timer or take as much time as you want or need. Ready? Here it is: If you could sit down next to Jesus today and talk about absolutely anything and everything, what would you talk about?

Establish: A Time to Build

Softly looking at ourselves does not mean glossing over our difficulties or faults. It means viewing ourselves through Christ's compassionate eyes. . . . Power comes from such true self-awareness.

Robert J. Wicks, *Availability*[17]

Find your authentic voice. As you move through the day or the week, think about and become increasingly aware of how you use your voice:

- Observe your use of verbal (words) and nonverbal (facial expressions, body movement/postures, gestures, eye contact, touch, space, tone of voice) language. As your self-awareness heightens, make a few notes about both the positives and the negatives and how you can do better. Remember, when we know better, we do better.
- What areas need improvement? Do you need to relax your facial muscles? Smile more? Soften your tone of voice?
- Where do you excel? Give yourself a little pat on the back. Go ahead. Even God stepped back from a hard day's work and saw that "it was very good" (Gen. 1:31 NIV).

Increased self-awareness is a valuable tool for living into your beautiful new story.

TOOL 6

Soak in Living Water

SPIRITUAL GROWTH*

THE INTENTION OF TOOL 6:

I soak in living water beliefs.*

I want first of all . . . to be at peace with myself. I want a singleness of eye, a purity of intention, a central core to my life that will enable me to carry out these obligations and activities as well as I can. I want, in fact—to borrow from the language of the saints—to live 'in grace' as much of the time as possible. I am not using this term in a strictly theological sense. By grace I mean an inner harmony, essentially spiritual, which can be translated into outward harmony. I am seeking perhaps what Socrates asked for in the prayer from the Phaedrus when he said, 'May the outward and inward man be one.' I would like to achieve a state of inner spiritual grace from which I could function and give as I was meant to in the eye of God.

Anne Morrow Lindbergh, *Gift from the Sea*

W
e were in the middle of yet another riveting soul-searching meeting when I noticed Laura's eyes look over my shoulder.

"Do you think they can hear us?" she asked.

I nonchalantly turned my head to check the distance between our tables.

"Oh, no," I said and smiled at her. "I think we are good. But I'll tone it down, just in case."

You see, when Laura and I meet, which is typically bimonthly in her favorite office-space-away-from-home, our conversations get really deep, really fast.

To those around us, Laura might appear to be only a young woman in a wheelchair—unable to pick up her own cup of coffee or walk to the restroom on her own. But to me, her friend and life coach, she is a marvel—a remarkable, inspiring, highly intelligent, richly gifted woman with great big dreams.

The last time we were together, we explored the subject of being an inspiration, particularly focusing on her latest writing projects about the misconceptions surrounding disability. The question at hand this day was, "Are we [the physically disabled] inspirations for simply living with a disability in the day-to-day? Just the sheer fact that we get out of bed and live our days confined by disability? Why is that so inspiring?" She was frustrated, in a good way, and baffled at how she and her disability inspire others.

I see Laura as an inclusion architect. She uses her frustrations and personal challenges to make the world a better, safer place for all beings, disabled or able-bodied. Much like a builder or architect designs a home or building with disability access, Laura longs to design emotional-health access and healthy inclusion for the disabled.

We looked at inspiration from a multitude of different angles. We tried to examine the perceptions of various observers—children, adults, strangers, peers. Our passion-o-meter needle went way to the right and brought us to one strong conclusion: we should all be inspiring one another as we do life together.

"You inspire me, Laura, because every single morning you wake up and face your arthrogryposis[1] with vigor and courage," I said. "I inspire you because I work, study, and help women find their full potential."

Inspiration encompasses every single person on the face of the earth—the disabled and the able-bodied.

We ended our conversation with the biggest question of all: Aren't we all disabled in some way?

One definition of *disability* puts it this way: impaired or limited by "a physical, mental, cognitive, or developmental condition."[2] (Note the word *cognitive*, as we'll be coming back to this critical aspect of disability.) When you look at disability from this angle, it seems to be more universal. Because of her fancy wheelchair, Laura's disability is more obvious and more noticeable in public. It is much easier to move through a room with less visible disabilities, such as depression or anxiety, as they can be more private in nature. They might make a person look sad or down, but that person wouldn't be labeled as "disabled."

"Think of it this way," Laura said. "Both of us can be inspired to keep going forward in life—to keep reaching for the next normal thing or the next impossible dream."

"Yes!" I shouted, quickly gaining my composure and lowering my voice to not embarrass Laura. "That is the real bottom line, isn't it?"

Limitless Laura

The first time I met Laura, I knew she was a remarkable human being who had the fight and fury of an overcomer inside of her. In her mind, she is 100 percent capable of doing anything and everything. She sees no limitations whatsoever. She accepts no sympathy—it kind of frustrates her—nor does she want any special treatment. She is her own woman. I suspect that her parents and two older brothers did such a great job of empowering her that she truly doesn't see that her life isn't normal.

I clearly remember the defining moment when I had to gently, yet firmly, break the news to her that she is indeed different. Her brow crinkled, her head tilted, and her eyes seemed to say, "I'm not really sure what you mean. How am I different?" In that moment, my deep admiration and respect for her transformed into sheer inspiration. She sees no limitations, even though she is highly limited, at least physically. For that reason alone, I couldn't help but tell her what an inspiration she is to me.

"But I'm just being me. Why is that so inspiring?" she asked, half smiling, wanting desperately to be inspiring for being herself, not her disabled self.

"Laura, let's take a closer look at the root word of inspiration, *inspire*," I said, taking my phone out of my bag. "I think it's worth our time."

"Inspire" comes from the Latin *inspirare*, meaning "breathe or blow into. The word was originally used of a divine or supernatural being, in the sense 'impart a truth or idea to someone.'"[3] Could we say that to inspire or be an actual inspiration to others simply looks like breathing truth? Breathing ideas? Breathing new life into the world around us?

Cognitive Disabilities: Mental Thorns

Laura breathes truth and fresh ideas into my life every time we meet, particularly when we talk about limits and limitations and how they relate to mental and emotional boundaries. She surprises me and challenges my preconceived notions about disability and what it means to be disabled. Her capacity to push beyond the limitations her physical body puts on her astonishes me.

Laura and I both agreed that as difficult as physical disabilities are, it is also difficult to have cognitive disabilities—that is, mental disabilities or, as some say, mental handicaps or limitations. These disabilities are challenging because they are invisible to the naked eye. Can you

- put a brace or cast on your mind?
- put a sling on the prefrontal cortex?
- stitch up an emotional wound?
- detect the shame folded into neural pathways?
- bind a grudge with butterfly closure strips?
- give your heart crutches and tell it not to put any weight on itself for six weeks?

We can head to our new mental gym and implement our heart-lifting workout, but in general, there aren't many, if any, actual spaces or places to develop and strengthen emotional health. It is a tough subject to broach. Traditionally, conversations about our emotional health happen inside a counseling or therapy office, but my hope is we can expand this conversation beyond those walls and into the hallways of our homes and churches. Practicing psychotherapist Richard Winter refers to these cognitive disabilities/

difficulties as "mental thorns." In his theological discussion about human suffering, *The Roots of Sorrow*, he writes, "It's perhaps easier to come to terms with an obvious physical disability such as being born with only one arm. You know what you have to accept, and you know your limitations. But when it comes to psychological disabilities, what I would call mental thorns, they are not so easy to define, and we do not know how much they will change in this life. Through our weakness, through the brokenness of our bodies and minds, God is working out his purpose of changing us into his image."[4]

Not So Easy to Define

"Mental thorns" are not so easy to define. *Limit* and *limitation* often have a negative connotation, but when fully understood, they are incredibly liberating. First, a quick glance at the meaning of *limit*, *limitation*, and *unlimited*:

A limit (n) is "a point or level beyond which something does not or may not extend or pass; the furthest extent of one's physical or mental endurance; a restriction on the size and amount of something permissible or possible."[5]

A limitation (n) is "a limiting rule or condition; a restriction; a shortcoming or defect."[6]

Unlimited (adj) is "having no restrictions or controls; having or seeming to have no boundaries; infinite; without qualification or exception; absolute: *unlimited confidence*."[7] Some synonyms are inexhaustible, boundless, immense, vast, great.

Once we come to terms with our humanity, we can begin practicing the skillful art of setting healthy emotional limits and limitations, known in the psychological realm as healthy mental, emotional, and relational boundaries. Often, the hardest part of writing and living into a new narrative is coming to terms with our personal mental thorns—our cognitive limitations—and discerning where, when, and how to establish healthy boundaries.

Volumes have been written on the important role of healthy boundaries in our lives,[8] yet it remains a common problem. There is a great tension involved in accepting our human limitations and then setting mental boundaries, especially within our closest relationships. This has been one of the most difficult parts of my own journey toward wholeness: learning to say no, recognizing I can't do it all and that I am not supposed to, and understanding my value in order to use my voice. I have learned the hard way that everyone's business is *actually* not my business (1 Thess. 4:11–12).

In the Judeo-Christian worldview, we are often told to love without limits. But we struggle to apply the principle in real life:

- Turn the other cheek? (Matt. 5:39)
- Give until it hurts? (Luke 6:32-36)
- Love my enemy? (Matt. 5:43–48)
- Forgive and forget? (Col. 3:13)
- Not help someone who needs me? (Luke 5:16)

The answer to these difficult questions is both yes and no, which challenges us to wrestle with the mystery involved in answering them. In truth, my own wrestling match with them has led me to write this book. I wholeheartedly believe that strong emotional health leads to authentic spiritual formation. When

I am emotionally healthy, I give and love and serve freely, albeit sacrificially at times (Eph. 5:1-2), because my value, worth, and dignity are not attached to "what I do" but to "who I am." When I am emotionally unhealthy, I create disordered attachments.[9] I'm giving and doing out of my deep unhealthy need for acceptance, applause, approval, or acknowledgement. In this scenario, I am desperately trying to be seen and loved for the wrong reasons—because of *what I do* and not for *who I am*. I'm trying to fill that gaping hole inside my insecure attachment (see Tool 2), and this often results in confusion, anger, bitterness, unforgiveness, danger-ous emotional and relational fatigue, and sadly, spiritual burnout. In her bestselling book *Braving the Wilderness*, Brené Brown asks:

> Where is the line? Is there a line in the wilderness between what behavior is tolerable and what isn't? The reward may be great, but do I have to put up with someone tearing me down or questioning my actual right to exist? Is there a line that shouldn't be crossed? The answer is yes. In my research, the clearer and more respected the boundaries, the higher the level of empathy and compassion for others. Fewer, clear boundaries, less openness. It's hard to stay kind-hearted when you feel people are taking advantage of you or threatening you. There is a line. It's etched from dignity.[10]

A Line Etched from Dignity

Dignity is one of the foundational principles of the Heartlift Method and our heartlifting journey toward emotional health and wellness. God breathed his life and virtue into us (Gen. 2:7); we have value, worth, and dignity. This truth serves as the founda-tion of how we live, move, and have our being. It informs every relationship we have, whether with close family members or with complete strangers.

As we move forward, keep this thought in mind: heartlifters treat everyone in their spheres of influence with value, worth, and dignity. Author Donna Hicks writes:

> Dignity is our inherent value and worth as human beings; everyone is born with it. Everyone recognizes that we all have a deep, human desire to be treated as something of value. I believe that is the highest common denominator. This shared desire for dignity transcends all of our differences, putting our common human identity above all else. While our uniqueness is important, history has shown us that if we don't take the next step toward recognizing our shared identity, conflicts in our workplace, our personal lives, and between nations will continue to abound. The glue that holds all of our relationships together is the mutual recognition of the desire to be seen, heard, listened to, and treated fairly; to be recognized, understood, and to feel safe in the world.[11]

Creating Safe Places and Spaces

Schools, workplaces, and shopping malls don't feel like safe places anymore. What should we do: Live in fear? Stay inside? No. We can't let fear win. God intends life to be lived (John 10:10), and he empowers us to do just that (2 Tim. 1:7). With faith and prayer, hard work and heartlifting practices, we can make our own little piece of the world a safe place to be. As we become emotionally healthy and spiritually authentic, we can influence others to do the same. Healthy begets healthy. Fear can be defeated by strong faith and a united (me + you = we) fervor for change.

Jesus mastered and modeled the methodology of creating safe places and spaces for people. As we see with the Samaritan woman, he goes out of his way to do so. John 4:4 says, "Now he had to go through Samaria" (NIV). Samaria wasn't a welcoming place for Jesus, but he knew there was a woman who needed his presence and a heartlift in her life. He knew there was a community that needed heartlifting—that is, healing, hope, and restoration.

When he meets the Samaritan woman, she is bound in her own limiting belief system. Maybe she put herself under the dominion of self-made limitations. Perhaps a mother or father, siblings, partners, peers, culture, or an unhealthy religious system spoke limits over her, and she allowed them to do so (whether this was a conscious decision or not). Maybe she absorbed limiting beliefs from an unhealthy emotional atmosphere in her family of origin. Maybe she didn't know a way out, felt stuck or numb or truly hopeless: *This is the way it has always been, and it won't change. This is my lot in life. Deal with it.* We aren't privy to any formative information about her. What kind of home life did she have? Did she experience a rough childhood? Was she bullied? What happened to diminish her sense of self? Regardless, she meets this man called Jesus, and he confronts her limiting beliefs—with love and authority. He acknowledges that she's been married five times.

- Why is that?
- What are you looking for?
- Is your life meaningful?
- Why are you allowing, giving permission, and even standing for so little when I have so much more?
- Why do you consistently sell yourself short and diminish your value, worth, and dignity?

Limiting Beliefs or Living Water?

Jesus shows this woman unlimited, lavish grace and offers her unlimited access to his living water—not just a potful but inexhaustible living water that would never, ever stop flowing in her soul and in her life. Jesus says to her, "If you knew the gift of God and who it is that asks you for a drink, you would have asked him and he would have given you living water" (John 4:10 NIV). He describes this living water as "a spring of water [satisfying his thirst for God] welling up [continually flowing, bubbling within him] to eternal life" (John 4:14 AMP).

At first, disbelief overwhelms her. *How can this be? What on earth is he talking about? Living water? Welling up within me? What on earth does that even mean? I just want one pot of water. That's all.* She is confounded and captivated all at the same time. She can't understand such an invitation. Never in her life has she been invited to the party. Never has she felt as if she truly fit in or even dared feel as if she belonged. Never has she experienced this type of unconditional love. She lived her life armored up, but now, the armor is falling off her, piece by piece.

We all have a belief system. "Beliefs are literally the lens through which you view the world,"[12] writes author Steve Sisgold. Beliefs are complex; they define us and organize our worlds. They can also

- influence perceptions
- define what is good, bad, true, real, or possible
- skew perspective in positive or negative ways
- direct and/or limit the actions you take
- shape character
- affect relationships

- establish a specific course or path for your life
- determine your health
- harness or hijack passion
- lower or raise your level of happiness or, may I add, meaningfulness[13]

Living into our beautiful new story requires that we define our belief system and, for the sake of our work here, define our unhealthy limiting belief systems.[14] Look at the list below. Circle or highlight any that resonate with you. Consider the source of your limiting belief. Maybe another one rose up in your heart. Write that in the blanks provided.

- Nobody cares what I have to say.
- I am good but not good enough.
- I'll never be as smart as she is.
- If only I were thinner or taller.
- I'm not worth it.
- Nothing will change.
- It's always been this way.
- It's too hard to change.
- No one will ever be interested in me.
- I'll be happy when I _____.
- Who would want to hire me? Marry me? Date me? Publish me? _____ me?
- I'm a procrastinator. Always have been, always will be.
- I can't because I _____.
- Whatever will be, will be.

- I can't. .
- I don't have enough support.
- Why even try?

Like the Samaritan woman, I believe that Jesus gives us a choice: Will your life continue to be dictated by your limiting belief system *or* will you unleash the power of living water beliefs over and through your life? Today, which will it be?

Living Water Unleashes the Unlimited

When the Samaritan woman hears Jesus talk about living water, her excitement is almost palpable. "Sir," she says, "give me some of that water! Then I'll never be thirsty again and won't have to make this long trip out here every day" (John 4:15 TLB). Did she even know what she was asking for? I'm not sure. But she knew she had to have it.

Living water unleashes unlimited resources for living *eudamonia*—the meaningful life we all deeply long for. Living, or *zaō* [15] in the Greek, means "to enjoy real life, . . . to be in full vigour [active bodily or mental strength or force], . . . to be fresh, strong, efficient." [16] Wow. Who doesn't want this kind of life? I know I do, and I'm 100 percent confident that you do too. Your thirst for more has led you right here.

My limiting belief system. ⟩ Jesus unleashes his unlimited *zaō*-charged resources. ⟩ Now, I live with living water beliefs.

Today, Jesus offers you living water. Bring him the limiting beliefs of your old narrative, ones learned, either consciously or subconsciously, in unhealthy systems. Let. them. go. Release each one of them and receive the refreshing renewal of his living water. From this moment forward, live a life of unlimited living water, *zaō*-charged resources. Jesus sets us free, offers sound principles that promise a meaningful life (limits set by his love and wisdom), and lavishes each one of us, his cherished children, with unlimited resources to flourish.

Strength Training for the Soul

Today's Heartlift: "Spirituality* is about seeing. It's not about earning or achieving. It's about relationship rather than results or requirements. Once you see, the rest follows. You don't need to push the river, because you are in it. The life is lived within us, and we learn how to say yes to that life. If we exist on a level where we can see how 'everything belongs,' we can trust the flow and trust the life, the life so large and deep and spacious that it even includes its opposite, death. We must do this, because it is the only life available to us, as Paul wrote to the Colossians, 'You have died [the small ego* self], and the life you now have is hidden with Christ in God [the Godself]. When Christ is revealed—*and he is your life*—you too will be revealed in all your glory with him' (Col. 3:3–4)."

Richard Rohr, *Everything Belongs*[17]

Envision: A Time to Think

The Samaritan woman's limiting belief system kept her bound to a lesser life—a life of settling, not a life lived more abundantly (John 10:10). Instead of pursuing meaningfulness, she remained stuck. Maybe she didn't know any better, but we do. Deep down in our heart of hearts we know there is "more" and "better" and even "best." Within the entire text of the Bible, we have unlimited access to God's beautiful, unlimited living water, *zaō*-charged resources— his powerful principles and purposes for living a rich, meaningful life. With unlimited access to television, podcasts,[18] and websites, helpful resources are just a click away (several ideas are presented in the next section, "Educate: A Time to Learn"). In the chart below, make note of your limiting beliefs (I'm sharing one of mine as an example) and then let Jesus unleash his living water over that belief. Let's call this forward movement "Let the Living Water Flow."

Limiting Beliefs	Living Water Beliefs
I am good, but not good enough.	Ephesians 2:10, "For we are the product of His hand, heaven's poetry etched on lives, created in the Anointed, Jesus, to accomplish the good works God arranged long ago." *God created me to offer good things in my sphere of influence.*

Educate: A Time to Learn

Change is hard work. Sometimes it seems easier just to ignore hurtful words or bad behaviors. But ask yourself, *Is it really easier? Won't I eventually pay the price of suppressing or repressing negative emotions?* Numbing negative emotions eventually takes its toll.

In his insightful book *Everything Belongs*, author and spiritual writer Richard Rohr offers these words:

> Many others give up their boundaries before they have them, always seeking their identity in another group, experience, possession, or person. Beliefs like, "She will make me happy," or "He will take away my loneliness," or "This group will make me feel like I belong" become a substitute for doing the hard work of growing up. . . .
>
> People who have learned to live from their center in God know which boundaries are worth maintaining and which can be surrendered, although it is this very struggle that often constitutes their deepest "dark nights."[19]

Rohr reiterates the power of setting intentional mental and emotional boundaries. Over the next seven days, choose one—just one—of your limiting belief entries in the "Envision" exercise. Spend time and valuable emotional energy researching and listening to or reading additional materials that can help you drown the limited belief with the living water promised to you by Jesus himself (John 4:14). Use the following chart to help you:

From Limiting Beliefs to Living Water Beliefs	I did it!
1. Search the internet by putting in key words from your limiting belief. For example: Limiting belief: *I am good, but not good enough.* Search: *Why do I feel "not good enough"?* Articles, YouTube talks, presentations, and much more come right up. Choose one or two to read, watch, or listen to. Write one truth in your journal.	
2. Search online for applicable podcasts or other interesting website(s) that can offer additional helpful resources.	
3. Find one Scripture verse or passage that can guide your prayers and meditation.	
4. Set an alarm at noon (on your phone, computer, or alarm clock) to remind you—halfway through your day—to check in with yourself and see how you are doing. We'll talk more about this in Tool 7.	

Establish: A Time to Build

Today, as you take time to build, read through or listen to the audio-meditative exercise "Come, Sit by the Well" (at www.janell rardon.com) and allow the words to have their full effect. As you listen, consider *unlimited* in this frame: *God's living water has no restrictions or boundaries. It is infinitely available to you.* I created this meditation with one intention: that all your limiting beliefs be completely drowned in the *zaō*-charged vigorous flow of living water.

Find a quiet spot. Give yourself the gift of a few minutes. Listen for God-whispers. Put on your headphones and let the noise of the world around you fade away. Let the same Jesus who sat at the Samaritan well unleash his unlimited love and grace on you as he did for the Samaritan woman so long ago. He is the same yesterday, today, and forever (Heb. 13:8).

Come, Sit by the Well

Come, sit by the well.
You've had a long journey, and I know you are tired.
I've seen your tears and heard your weeping.
You thought no one cared. No one understood. No one
saw how hard you were trying.
I care. I understand. I see your efforts. Most importantly, I
know your heart.
I see you.
I destined this exact moment for you.
Today is your day.
Today, I want to ask you to do something for me. It's
different and might be shocking, but it will bring you to
your deepest desire and unfulfilled longing.
The one that you've been afraid to even voice.
The one you've whispered on your pillow at night.

Come, sit by the well.
Today, I want you to stop trying so hard to be perfect.
Stop trying to make everyone happy.
Stop trying to make me proud.
You are enough. Just like you are.
You can never disappoint me, fail me, or cause me to leave
your side.
Today, I want to put a skip back in your step.
Today, I want to help you giggle and laugh and find joy in
the simplest of pleasures.
Start leaning hard on me.
Start trusting that I love you just the way I created you.
Nothing more. Nothing less.

Come, sit by the well.
You are enough. Just like you are.

Receive my living water.
Let it wash over you like a refreshing summer shower.
Live in its ebb and flow.
At times you will have to be patient, as a season of
    spiritual drought or dryness may come.
At times you will be carried along by its current.
At times you will rest by its riverbank.
But always, come, sit by the well.

Meditative Response: Did you hear any God-whispers? Did he speak between the lines as you listened? When you heard "You are enough. Just like you are," how did that make you feel? Yes, feel. Somatic experience—that is, self-awareness of sensory affects in your body—is vital to writing a new narrative. For example, when I heard the words "You are enough. Just like you are," I felt my shoulders relax. They actually moved from a high position to a relaxed position. I sank into my chair. I felt lighter and brighter as a physical release moved me from being so tightly wound. I finally understood what relaxing feels like.

PART THREE

Establish

ESTABLISH (v): To found, institute, build, or bring into being on a firm or stable basis.

> Your hands have made me and established me;
> Give me understanding and a teachable heart,
> that I may learn your commandments.
>
> Psalm 119:73 AMP

TOOL 7

Send New, Positive Messages to Your Brain

MEMORY RECONSOLIDATION

THE INTENTION OF TOOL 7:
I send new, positive messages to my brain.

Denial of one's need for others is the most common type of defense against bonding. If people come from a situation, whether growing up or later in life, where good, safe relationships were not available to them, they learn to deny that they even want them. Why want what you can't have? They slowly get rid of their awareness of the need.

Henry Cloud, *Changes That Heal: How to Understand Your Past to Ensure a Healthier Future* t was Mother's Day, a day typically celebrated with church services, family gatherings, fancy five-star brunches, kind words about the sacrifices and dedication of our mothers, and cards and gifts. But this year, in my family of origin, Mother's Day held gifts of another kind—hard conversations, emotional healing, and the promise of authentic sibling relationships. I could see it was going to be anything but *typical*.

Instead of spending it with my own children, I spent the day in a hospital room. I didn't want to be there. I wanted to fly all my children home and cook them a big family dinner. But this day would be about a long overdue, much-needed "gutting to the emotional bones" of my family of origin.

It's about We

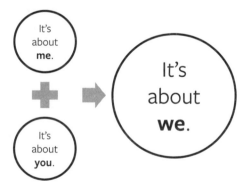

The emotional temperature in the room was rising. My older sister, Susan, and I stood at the foot of our ninety-year-old mother's hospital bed. Much like the woman with the issue of blood (Luke 8:43–48), our mother, too, had an issue of blood that wouldn't relent. Five years prior to this medical crisis, she had come very close to death due to the same chronic condition.

Yet she lived.

Now, death was knocking on her door once again. The past eight days had been laden with 911 emergency calls, near-death experiences, and repetitive tests and examinations by a host of hospitalists and medical specialists. Each day seemed to repeat the previous one: bleeding scans, multiple CTs, blood transfusions, and cardiac assessments. Our mother needed a major high-risk surgery—one that a typical person her age would rarely survive, according to statistics.

Repeatedly, I told the doctors, "You don't know my mother. She left her family home in Wisconsin to join the marines. She was a member of the First Battalion of Women Marines on Parris Island in 1949. If anyone will survive it, she will. At eighty-two years old, she endured brain surgery and didn't even get a headache. My mother is tough."

Doctors were reluctant and rightly so. She was ninety and seemingly fragile.

Family, friends, and communities of faith were praying. My mother's prayer was simple and direct: "God, I need a small miracle."

One surgeon decided he would give her a second look. He scheduled an emergency surgical procedure for Mother's Day in hopes of finding some hidden source of bleeding. One that would be easier to fix or at least easier for her to manage.

We waited hours for the surgeon to arrive on the scene. The stress of the past week had left each of us hanging on the edge of our last nerve. Fatigue disables emotion regulation and, in ever-so-subtle fashion, drains the nervous system of coping strategies and defense mechanisms. All three of us wanted to be anywhere but in room 557.

Psychologists would say our "window of tolerance"*[1] was slowly but surely getting to the point of being completely closed. We were doing our best to manage the strain, but the emotional atmosphere was thick with frustration, fear, and the emergence of decades-long family grievances. On top of this, the relationships of the three women in the room were affected by the unhealthy behavior patterns of triangulation,* favoritism,* and comparison.*

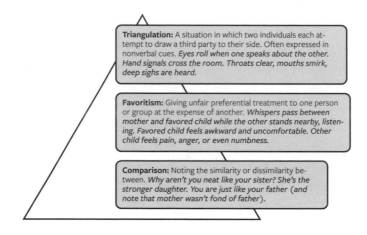

Triangulation: A situation in which two individuals each attempt to draw a third party to their side. Often expressed in nonverbal cues. *Eyes roll when one speaks about the other. Hand signals cross the room. Throats clear, mouths smirk, deep sighs are heard.*

Favoritism: Giving unfair preferential treatment to one person or group at the expense of another. *Whispers pass between mother and favored child while the other stands nearby, listening. Favored child feels awkward and uncomfortable. Other child feels pain, anger, or even numbness.*

Comparison: Noting the similarity or dissimilarity between. *Why aren't you neat like your sister? She's the stronger daughter. You are just like your father (and note that mother wasn't fond of father).*

Timing Is Everything

At the height of the increasing tension, my older brother, Mike, who lived about three hours away, called to check in. I filled him in on the unfolding medical drama and gave him the recent updates.

After we briefly talked, he asked to speak to my older sister.

"Don't take any 'you-know-what' from Mom," he said to Susan. "Don't internalize anything she says to you right now. Let it roll off your back."

Talk about timing. Not only were his words timely, they were also very precious to my sister. You see, at the time, my older brother and sister were suffering with a heartrift. They'd been struggling in their sibling relationship, as we all do from time to time, and they needed some emotional healing.

Add to typical sibling conflict the additional strain of having been raised in the home of an alcoholic. As adult children of an alcoholic father (ACOA), we've had our fair share of relational struggles. The American Addiction Center writes, "Substance abuse affects a family on every level: emotional, psychological, financial, and social. Worst of all, addiction undermines the loving, trusting relationships that sustain a healthy family. Restoring those relationships, which were often damaged long before the substance abuse began, requires time, patience, and the support of knowledgeable addiction professionals."[2]

Sadly, as children, we were not offered "the support of knowledgeable addiction professionals." I have no doubt my mother was doing her best just to keep the family fed, dressed, schooled—and together. Counseling—that is, talking about our problems—was not the accepted norm, nor was it easily accessible or affordable for an enlisted military family.

So as I sat in my uncomfortable hospital chair, watching and listening to the two of them talk, I felt immense gratitude. *Look at this,* I thought. *This is a small miracle, an answered prayer. It took Mom's medical trauma to begin mending their relationship, but to God be the glory. Mom asked for a small miracle and got something far greater than she knew.* This was a turn-it-around moment in the life of her children (Gen. 50:20), and boy was it a good one. Not your typical Mother's Day gift, but then again, this was no ordinary day.

When they were done talking, I looked at my sister and asked, "Wow, that was pretty special, right?"

"Surprising and very welcome," she said. "It felt good to talk and connect with my big brother again."

"Happy Mother's Day," I said. "Something good is coming out of all this drama."

Time passed ever so slowly as we continued to wait for the arrival of the surgeon. Mom started talking to Susan and me about the "new diet" her doctors said she would have to follow. Due to her highly challenged gastrointestinal system, she had been on a full-liquid diet for a couple of days. We weren't sure how long that would last, but the lack of food was making Mom a bit tense.

Mom was hungry, or should I say "hangry." I tried understanding her angst: "If only I could have some fried rice . . . all I want is a big bowl of buttered popcorn . . . a juicy hamburger sounds so good right now. Why can't I have these foods anymore? What will they actually do to me?"

At this point, Mom was dealing with loss on a grand scale: the recent loss of her car, loss of her mobility, loss of her condo, and more than anything, loss of her "oomph," or her "moxie," as they say. After moving into an assisted living facility, she missed her independence and was experiencing extended periods of grief over her diminishing capacity to do for herself. Now that I have adult children, I understand the tension in this phase of parenting. Do we, as *parents*, like the role reversal of having our children tell us how we should live?

As my sister and I earnestly, yet maybe a bit on the pushy, annoying side, went on about the list of should-nots, her anxiety level rose. When we mentioned that chocolate was a should-not, she grimaced. With so much already being taken away from her, did chocolate really have to be a should-not?

"I guess I can't have that anymore, right?" she asked—for the millionth time. "Not even a little tiny piece?" while motioning an inch-long air picture with her thumb and forefinger.

My sister and I looked at each other in utter exasperation, patience wearing thin. Trying to lighten the tension, Susan laughed and said, "Oh, Mom, go ahead, buy a big ole Hershey bar," motioning a foot-long air picture with her two hands.

Bad idea. The humor was lost on our hangry, frustrated, very ill mom.

"Stop being such a smart aleck!" my mother chided in a harsh tone.

The tenor and tone of the room immediately changed. I gasped, my sister sank a little deeper into her uncomfortable hospital chair, and my mother threw her head back onto her pillow and shut her eyes.

When the Trigger Alarm Sounds

An unhealthy trigger—the harsh, demeaning tone of my mother's voice—sounded from deep within my soul and my subconscious, where an emotionally charged childhood memory still resided. Immediately, with no warning, I froze. I felt emotionally unsafe. I wanted to run out of the room and out of the hospital. Much like an alarm rings to warn a community about an impending tornado, an emotional alarm went off inside of me.

I looked at my mother in disbelief.

I looked at my sister, exchanging a glance of bewilderment. *What just happened?*

"Mom!" I said. "Really?"

And then I was silent.

I reverted to my go-to defense mechanism—repression, or as we call it in my family, "the shutdown." This emotional reaction is not pretty and is very unhealthy. It causes hurt and emotional wounding, and it can have damaging physical repercussions too.[3] It is also something I am 100 percent committed to reframing and re-authoring in my life. But at this moment in time, it was an automatic reflex. *Shut down. You are not safe.* An iron door quickly closed over my heart.

Susan, on the other hand, took a few breaths and started talking about something else. In sheer admiration, I watched her continue to serve our mother. She picked up a brush and started fixing Mom's hair, making sure she looked presentable for the surgeon. Then she tidied up her bedside table and fluffed the pillow behind her head.

"Are you comfortable, Mom?" she asked. "Is there anything else I can do?"

My mother shook her head no and said, "Thank you."

Finally, the surgeon arrived, the procedure was completed, and results were in. Mom needed the high-risk surgery.

We had a very big decision to make.

Taking the Tension Out of Triggers

Let's face it. Conflict happens—especially in emotionally charged circumstances. In extreme times, triggers occur and defense mechanisms are activated, usually wrapped in tension and armed for a fight—either verbally (hurtful and hateful) or nonverbally (silent and unsafe).

A trigger is something that "sets off a memory tape or flashback, transporting the person back to the event of her/his original trauma."[4] Typically, they are unexpected, negative in nature, and take us completely off guard: a sudden jarring word is spoken, a nasty glare is given, someone rubs us the wrong way, a photo is posted on social media. Sometimes, however, they are pleasant, such as a surprise raise at work, someone speaking healing words that uplift, or friends showing up at your front door with flowers and balloons—just because.

Triggers can be counterproductive and draining, stir our competitive instincts, and so much more. For our purpose here, we are looking at triggers that lead to intensified, negative emotional reactions, the unhealthy ones that bind and breed even more unhealthy outcomes.[5]

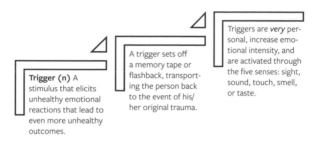

Trigger (n) A stimulus that elicits unhealthy emotional reactions that lead to even more unhealthy outcomes.

A trigger sets off a memory tape or flashback, transporting the person back to the event of his/her original trauma.

Triggers are *very* personal, increase emotional intensity, and are activated through the five senses: sight, sound, touch, smell, or taste.

Conflict is a major part of life and an integral part of relationships (with God, self, and others) and community (family, church, workplace, school, and so on), yet we are often not trained in healthy conflict-management skills. For many of us, triggers will come, so why not be prepared for them? How do we take the tension out of triggers in order to maintain a healthy emotional atmosphere in the room?

One of Jesus's closest friends, John, left us this message: "I have told you these things, so that in Me you may have [perfect] peace. In the world you have tribulation and distress and suffering, but be courageous [be confident, be undaunted, be filled with joy];

I have overcome the world" (John 16:33 AMP). Keeping John's words in the front of our minds, consider these tough questions:

- What do we do when conflict catches us off guard and triggers something subconsciously buried deep within our brains—even our nervous systems?
- How do we overcome our old narrative's bad habits?
- How do we make triggers work for us and not against us?
- How do we practice awareness of and respect the differences of others?
- How do we develop and practice the skill of healthy assertiveness (see Tool 5) and confront the person who sets the trigger in motion in a healthy manner that promotes positive outcomes and future freedom for the relationship?
- How do we identify unhealthy coping strategies learned during childhood?
- How do we move forward if the person pulling the trigger doesn't want to talk about it?
- How do we change negative-thought feedback loops and create new positive-thought feedback loops?
- If triggers are often linked to our defense mechanisms, is it possible to disarm unhealthy defense mechanisms and re-author them?

Detecting and Disarming our Defense Mechanisms

Typically, a trigger causes a flashback to a traumatic event in our past and activates our defense mechanisms in order to help us cope. Coping skills enable us to get through tough situations.[6]

Remember, triggers are highly individual. In fact, each of the nine Enneagram personality types have their very own dominant defense mechanism or defense system.[7]

You might ask, *What are defense mechanisms?*

In simplest terms, defense mechanisms, often called "ego defenses," are "psychological strategies that are unconsciously used to protect a person from anxiety arising from unacceptable thoughts or feelings. . . . We use defense mechanisms to protect ourselves from feelings of anxiety or guilt, which arise because we feel threatened or because our id or superego becomes too demanding."[8] They are not under our conscious control and are non-voluntaristic.

Bottom line? Defense mechanisms are natural God-given ways of coping with anything that threatens our physical or emotional safety. When someone or something makes us feel unsafe, our defense mechanisms kick in. We sometimes depend on them in unhealthy ways. Instead of getting to the "why" we feel unsafe, we get stuck. This keeps us from living a meaningful life.

One great way to rise above—or as we say in the Heartlift Method, "elevate the atmosphere"[9]—is to become acutely aware of our personalized and comfortable go-to defense mechanism(s) in order to detect it quickly and accurately. The key here is being "acutely aware." Knowledge is power, so let's empower ourselves by becoming acquainted with some of the most common defense mechanisms in order to identify which ones might be operating in our lives. I've added descriptions to the following chart to show what each one "looks like" and how it plays out in real life. Do any of them resonate within you?

Defense mechanism, often referred to as "ego defense"	How this plays out in families and relationships	One practice to make sure I am coping in a healthy, heartlifting way. This is personal.
1. Repression *Like an armadillo, you curl up in a ball and hide.*	Instead of using words/voice to speak unacceptable thoughts, feelings, or impulses, you swallow them and hide your true feelings.	I will use my words so that I no longer swallow unhealthy emotions that eventually will cause "dis-ease" in my physical body. There are physical consequences to storing repression inside my nervous system. I will always remember that God is the strength of my heart and that he will empower me to overcome.
2. Denial *Like an ostrich, you bury your head in the sand.*	Refusing to accept the reality of a situation, you treat it as if it doesn't exist. This denial is locked inside your nervous system and eventually causes havoc.	I will practice being present to my emotions, remembering that emotions are information. They help me process and live life from a healthy perspective.
3. Projection *Like a blue jay, you take out your negative feelings on others.*	You project or "place" your feelings on another person so that you don't have to "feel" or "deal" with them.	I will take complete ownership of my emotional reactions and do the hard work of processing and properly owning them.
4. Compartmentalization *Like a squirrel hides its nuts for the winter, you hide your feelings until later. You just can't deal with them right now.*	You subconsciously attempt to avoid cognitive dissonance or the mental discomfort and anxiety caused by a person who has conflicting values, cognitions, emotions, and beliefs within themselves.	I will practice mindfulness and self-awareness so that I can process my emotional state in a healthy manner and in a healthy time frame. As I recognize my tendency to avoid or delay the processing of my emotions, I will gain emotional health, which will result in relational health.
5. Intellectualization *Like an octopus can activate its high level of intelligence, you can do many things at one time. Yet you avoid any uncomfortable emotive response and process it intellectually instead. Your head overwhelms your heart, and your intellectualization is a transition to reason, whereby you avoid uncomfortable emotions and focus on facts and logic.*	You treat a situation as an interesting problem that engages you on a rational basis while completely ignoring the emotional aspects as being irrelevant.	I will value my capacity and ability to reason and problem solve while being present and self-aware of the emotions I am feeling in my body. Recognizing that emotions are energy in motion and that they inform my capacity and ability to reason enables me to process the emotions, not avoid them.
6. Regression *Like a baby kangaroo (a joey) nestling deep within its mother's pouch, maturity seems to poke at your comfort, asking you to learn mature coping skills. When emotions challenge, you tuck your head into the comforts of all you know.*	You abandon age-appropriate coping strategies in favor of earlier, more childlike patterns of behavior.	I will accept full responsibility for my personal growth and maturity, especially concerning my emotional and relational health. Instead of regressing or returning to "all I know," I will ask for help, seek counsel, or do whatever it takes to move forward into maturity.
7. Sublimation *Like a caterpillar that wrestles inside a restricting cocoon, you transform a negative into a positive.*	You take unacceptable impulses and transform them into acceptable expressions.	I will continue to seek ways to recognize, accept, and process the unacceptable or negative emotions I feel so that I can respond in a healthy emotional manner.

Heartlifters See from God's Vantage Point

My not-so-typical Mother's Day may have looked sad, unfortunate, or perhaps a bit gloomy, but seeing from God's vantage point—which is higher, wiser, and far better than ours—only good things, healthy things, were happening. Was it comfortable? No. Was it easy? No. But I sensed it was being divinely orchestrated, so I pressed on. Very often, a situation or circumstance *is being* orchestrated by God in order to bring much-needed healing and restoration. It looks and feels bad, sometimes really bad, in the moment, but it is ultimately very good (Gen. 50:20).

As heartlifters, we train ourselves to discern the tension between tender and tough love and pray through and stay with the conflict (see practice 4 in my book *Overcoming Hurtful Words*), diplomatically leading each party, much like a mediator would, to healthy responses and ultimately to a healthy resolution. In other words, heartlifters see relationships through to the end. When a heartlifter is at the center of a family, home is a safe, secure, and authentically spiritual place to be. Heartlifters keep the relational equation *you* + *me* = *we* front and center in their minds. Having experienced their own personal heartlift (me), they now have the enlarged capacity to offer those in their sphere of influence the power of their own heartlift (you), resulting in everyone (we) becoming emotionally healthy.

It seems the prophet Isaiah agrees with this idea. Isaiah was a heartlifter to God's people. He received a timeless message from God—one we need to tattoo across our hearts, especially during times of heightened, stress-laden relational conflict. When we want to storm out of a room, quit on our closest relationships, hurl hurtful words, or leave a family or community altogether, Isaiah's words guide us to take a deep breath, collect our strength, get our bearings, and activate the practice of heartlifting. He relays this message from God to us:

> My intentions are not always yours,
>> and I do not go about things as you do.
> My thoughts and My ways are above and beyond you,
>> just as heaven is far from your reach here on earth.
> For as rain and snow can't go back once they've fallen,
>> but soak into the ground
> And nourish the plants that grow,
>> providing seed to the farmer and bread for the hungry,
> So it is when I declare something.
>> My Word will go out and not return to Me empty,
> But it will do what I wanted;
>> it will accomplish what I determined.
> For you will go out in joy, be led home in peace.
>> And as you go the land itself will break out in cheers;
> The mountains and the hills will erupt in song,
>> and the trees of the field will clap their hands. (Isa. 55:8–12)

Heartlifters Commit to Progress, not Perfection

That defining moment when my hangry, frustrated mother harshly yelled at my sister, I shut down. My personal defense mechanism, repression, kicked into high gear. Instead of sending new, positive messages to my brain in order to elevate the atmosphere of the room, I voiced one sarcastic word, "Really?" I failed at implementing and practicing my own teaching. It was not my finest moment, but one of our community mantras is "progress, not perfection."

Every single failure is a step toward even greater understanding and, when examined, leads to personal growth.

As soon as the surgeon left, my sister and I packed up our things and said goodbye to Mom. We stood in the hospital parking lot for quite some time, taking a few deep breaths to rewind and reset the entire ordeal.

"I've never witnessed Mom act like that toward you," I said. "At least not that I remember. She was so harsh with you. How could you brush that off and then brush her hair? That is astounding to me."

"I'm used to it," my sister said. "She's talked to me that way my whole life. Being seven years younger than me, maybe you just don't remember."

"Well, that is not okay," I said. "She doesn't do that to me. She might feel like doing it, but she doesn't. Does Mom want her potential last words to you to be *those* words in *that* tone?

"We are better than this," I said. "It is time for a change. When we know better, we do better. Right?"

"Sadly, I know I've used that same harsh tone," my sister said, grimacing. "I don't want to do that anymore. I want to change."

"And I don't want to continue repressing my feelings," I said. "Repression has caused enough damage in my relationships. I'm so tired of the shutdown. It's taking a toll on my physical body too. I want to change."

Right then and there, my sister and I had our own special heartlift, committing to becoming stronger every day, to holding each other accountable, and to bracing ourselves on the bad days with healing words, unconditional love, sibling unity, and mutual respect and care.

Heartlifters Discern Kairos Time

Could I have been overreacting to my mom's harsh words to my sister? I hear all the voices—some in my head, some actually spoken to me: *Did you really say that to your mom? Lighten up, all families fight. Stop being so sensitive. She's ninety. Cut her some slack. Is that honoring your mother?*

I see and hear each and every comment.

But as a woman both personally and professionally committed to emotional health and wellness, I couldn't let the incident slide. There is a time to be silent and a time to speak (Eccles. 3:7). And, I believe, there is a healthy, heartlifting way to repair emotional wounds. This was not an offense I could or should overlook (Prov. 19:11). We needed an emotional repair in our family system. This was a God-breathed, *kairos* moment.

Isaiah 55:8–12 tells us that God's timing works on an entirely different system. A big part of living into your new story is both understanding and discerning this timing system. The ancient Greeks categorized time into two specific measures:

1. Chronos time: chronological, sequential "real time"—quantitative. Consider chronos time what we live in, day to day, a timing regulated by clocks and calendars.
2. Kairos time: a qualitative, more permanent "right time"—the critical or opportune moment. Consider kairos time as God's perfect timing, a timing that is harder to understand and more ethereal and eternal in nature. It is time from God's vantage point.

One of the foundational teachings on these two types of timing was written by wise King Solomon. In Ecclesiastes 3:1–8, he speaks of both chronos, real time, and kairos, the right time—showing us the importance of discerning between the two:

> For everything that happens in life—there is a season, a
>   right time for everything under heaven:
> A time to be born, a time to die;
>   a time to plant, a time to collect the harvest;
> A time to kill, a time to heal;
>   a time to tear down, a time to build up;
> A time to cry, a time to laugh;
>   a time to mourn, a time to dance;
> A time to scatter stones, a time to pile them up;
>   a time for a warm embrace, a time for keeping your
>   distance;
> A time to search, a time to give up as lost;
>   a time to keep, a time to throw out;
> A time to tear apart, a time to bind together;
>   a time to be quiet, a time to speak up;
> A time to love, a time to hate;
>   a time to go to war, a time to make peace.

There was no doubt in my mind that Mother's Day was the right, opportune, and highly critical time to heartlift my family of origin. Every single moment in my relationships with my mother and siblings led us to room 557. Like most families, we've endured many of the times Solomon speaks of—times of crying and times of laughter, times of mourning and times of dancing, times for warm embraces and times of keeping our distance, times of war and times of peace, times of being quiet and, now, times of speaking up.

True emotional healing was on the horizon, and everything up to this point had prepared "me" and "we" for this time.

Prosody: Peace, Power, or Poison?

What bothered me the most in that entire conflict was the harsh tone of my mother's voice. In counseling, we call tone of voice "prosody," a nonverbal communication skill that serves as the delivery system for our verbal communication. In the 1970s, professor emeritus and sociologist Albert Mehrabian "developed a communication model, in which he demonstrated that only 7% of what we communicate consists of the literal content of the message. The use of one's voice, such as tone, intonation and volume, take up 38% and as much as 55% of communication consists of body language. This 7–38–55 model is still much used today."[10] When it comes to healthy communication, what we say isn't as important as how we say it.

Prosody, like our words, holds either peace, power, or poison.

The morning after our "Mother's Day of Mayhem," I was scheduled to take my car into the collision center to be repaired. Just one day before my mom's medical crisis, my car was the third one in an ugly four-car pileup. On my way to a client session, I was driving along, enjoying the sunshine of the bright spring day. All of a sudden, I saw brake lights come on ahead and realized that a bright red construction truck had suddenly stopped, causing the two cars ahead of me, me, and a car behind me to slam on our brakes. Then a flash of red filled my rearview mirror as another bright red truck was coming up behind us. I knew if I didn't get out of the way, I would be sandwiched between two very big, very bright red trucks.

Somehow, within a millisecond, I looked ahead, decided where I could swerve safely, and got out of the way, landing on the double yellow lines in the middle of the road. Stunned, I sat in silence.

What do I do now? I came to my senses, found my phone, and called 911.

Miraculously, no one was badly hurt. Sore backs and tight necks, but thankfully, everyone walked away. Somehow, my car suffered only a big bang on the back bumper—yet needed a repair that was going to take about five days. At least I could drive it, so I made my way home.

Little did I know, at the time, how this accident foreshadowed the ensuing weeks.

Sometimes Heartlifters Have to Get Out of the Way

After dropping the car off at the collision center, I decided to swing by the hospital. It was early morning and time for a shift change, so time alone with Mom was a strong possibility. I wanted a kairos opportunity to talk to her about everything that had unfolded on Mother's Day. Not wanting to force the issue, I prayed that *if* it was the right time, the conversation would unfold naturally. Thankfully, it did.

It didn't take but a minute for her to comment on the previous day's situation. "You and your sister are so different," she said, shaking her head back and forth. "It's really unbelievable."

"Yes, we are," I said, taking in a very deep preparatory breath. "About that, Mom. Can I ask you something?"

I pulled my chair closer to her, leaned in, and rested my arms on the edge of her hospital bed. I took her hand in mine and got as close as I could.

"Mom," I said, "the past six years have been tough—on you, on me, on our family. You've been through so many serious medical crises, transitioned into assisted living, and lost so much, especially your independence. I can't imagine how traumatic all of this has been for you. During that time, we made a promise to hold one another accountable, to speak the truth in love, to be emotionally healthy," I said softly. "Do you remember that?"

"Yes, I do," she said. "That's why you write your books. That's why you help your ladies."

The next two hours were a gift from God. Just the two of us. With candor and respect, emotional repair took place. We were able to have a beautiful conversation about healthy communication.

"Thank you," she said, with a big smile on her face. "I owe you a check."

Our conversation and my mother's willingness to listen, learn, and hopefully love *better* was the lasting gift of this Mother's Day. Even at ninety years old, we can each move toward becoming our very best God-breathed "me," so we can ultimately become our very best God-breathed "we."

Strength Training for the Soul

Today's Heartlift: "So often change occurs from stories that we read, hear, or see, whether they include family legends, myths, fairy tales, novels, films, television shows, plays, song lyrics, or even blogs. It turns out that because of mirror neurons we can experience vicarious life events as if they really happened to us. As far as your brain is concerned, the people you 'meet' in stories really *are* your friends and loved ones. And the adventures you enjoy through fiction and stories really do teach you important lessons. . . . The strong emotions you feel during a well-told story further cement memory and help you to retrieve information in the future, all without leaving the safety and comfort of a chair."

Jeffrey A. Kottler[11]

Envision: A Time to Think

During my mother's medical crisis, she had one request: I need a small miracle. She repeated it over and over again. I kept wondering where the thought of only a "small" miracle was coming from. Is there any such thing as a "small" miracle? I didn't correct her, just agreed and prayed. But one morning as I was entering the hospital, I thought, *Ask for something greater. God is almighty. He wants us to ask for something greater than a "small" miracle.* So I asked.

As you pick up your pen today, read through or listen to the audio narration (see janellrardon.com/resources) of the following prayer and ask God for something greater—not just a small miracle but something far greater.

Great and mighty God,

Why do I ask for a small miracle when you can do so much more? Why do I place limits and boundaries on your capacity to bless? Am I afraid of being disappointed? Do I think I am unworthy? Do I doubt that you will help me? Do I have the wrong idea about your love or power?

Right now, I welcome you into all my whys.

Right now, I wholeheartedly seek the courage to ask for something greater.

Right now, I open my heart and hands—ready to embrace your healing words.

You tell me to ask, seek, and knock (Matt. 7:7–12), so I ask for something greater.

You tell me to embrace tests and hardships (James 1:2–4), so I ask for greater patience and strength so that my faith will blossom under the pressure.

You tell me that you are far greater than he who is in this world (1 John 4:4), so I believe that you are far greater and will help me overcome.

You tell me that if I believe in you, I will do even greater works than you (John 14:1–14), so I lay aside doubt and fear and place my trust in you.

You tell me that you are able to do far more abundantly than I can ask or think (Eph. 3:20), so today, I let go of any limitations or boundaries or small thinking that is keeping me from your great plan for my life.

You tell me that you have blessed me with every spiritual blessing in the heavenly places (Eph. 1:3), so I put away unhealthy beliefs, behaviors, and bad attitudes that keep me bound in discouragement, impoverishment, or self-pity.

You tell me I am loved with an everlasting love and that you have drawn me with unfailing kindness (Jer. 31:3), so I rest in the fact that you actually desire more for me than I do for myself.

You tell me I am stronger than I think (Phil. 4:13), and so I choose to wake up every single day of the rest of my life believing what you say about me.

I will grow stronger every day of my life.

Amen.

Educate: A Time to Learn

Did you know that there are over thirty-four thousand emotions? That's why it is critical that we get to know our emotions. Emotional literacy, "the ability to deal with one's emotions and recognize their causes,"[12] is central to living into our beautiful new story. Each of us has absorbed the atmosphere of our family of origin and picked up ways of coping that developed into our go-to defense mechanisms. Having a strong, solid emotional vocabulary helps us understand how to recognize, label, and navigate the eight primary emotions: joy, sadness, acceptance, disgust, fear, anger, surprise, and anticipation (and have a slight grasp of the other 33,992 others).[13] Author and international expert on leadership and human performance Dr. Alan Watkins writes:

> If we start to become much more precise in our emotional literacy, then we can come up with a more effective strategy for dealing with negative emotions and creating a positive emotional state. So, how do you feel good about yourself more often? It's perfectly possible, but it does require practice and it's not just about positive affirmation—telling yourself to feel happier or more confident doesn't work. Instead, you have to feel the emotion, feel the feeling, not just think the thought. For example, when you think about something positive in your life that gives you a positive feeling (or emotion), take time to consider exactly how you feel, where in your body you are feeling it, articulate the emotion—is it happiness, contentment, glee, delight? The more you practice feeling that feeling, the easier it will be to conjure up that emotion when you need it—even in the face of someone else trying to make you feel something more negative. You need to learn to control your response in whatever situation you find yourself—to become "response-able," that is, able to respond in the way you choose.[14]

Building an emotional vocabulary takes time. Treat this as if you were learning a second language. American psychologist Robert Plutchik developed a helpful tool called "The Wheel of Emotions."[15] See the following illustration.[16] Get to know these emotions and how they "look" in your life. Note the positive and the negative aspects of each emotional state.

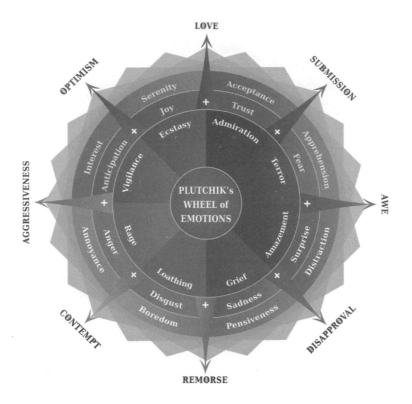

Remember these three things:

1. Emotions are vital information, potent energy in motion
   and important signals of very real "feelings" (in our physical bodies) that we need to recognize, label, navigate,
   and voice. Yes, we have to use our words. Maybe you've
   been taught that emotions are bad; maybe you've been
   repressed, silenced, or told to "just get over it"; or maybe
   you haven't been taught anything at all about how to handle or feel your emotions.

2. We control our emotions; they do not control us. There's a big difference. We ought to say, "I feel anger," not "I am angry."

3. Emotions are meant to be felt and regulated. Become really good friends with your new healthy emotional self.

The title of Tool 7 suggests sending a new message to your brain. To do so, you must take action steps and implement practices in your life. Start here and now. Take a pause midday to ask yourself a few questions: *How am I doing right now? How have I practiced detecting my defense mechanisms today? Has my awareness about my personal triggers increased?*

Establish: A Time to Build

Just as I finished this book and sent it to the publisher, a major delay occurred. Circumstances beyond my control unfolded, and I was devastated. At the time, *chronos* time, I couldn't understand what was happening. But six months later, in *kairos* time, it all became crystal clear. It wasn't God's time to release this book into the world. I had to get out of God's way and surrender to the movement of his Spirit. I had more to learn.

A friend invited me to attend an event that introduced me to a new and revolutionary emotional-health modality, the Aroma Freedom Technique, developed by clinical psychologist Benjamin Perkus in alignment with the research and writings of Gary Young, the father of the modern essential oil movement. This simple, safe, and highly efficient healing modality incorporates several different psychological therapies, including EMDR (eye movement desensitization and reprocessing), with the power of aromatherapy and the use of memory reconsolidation—the brain's natural way of updating and learning. Dr. Perkus discovered that "holding the four primary aspects of consciousness together at the same time (feeling, thought, sensation, and imagination) while smelling specific [strategically formulated therapeutic-grade] essential oils had the effect of 'dissolving' the memory/emotion complex and allowed the person to become free from the effects of negative experiences from the past."[17]

Through the years, I have had many clients who remained stuck in unhealthy behavior patterns. They kept tripping over the same root, no matter how hard we worked to dig it out. We couldn't resolve the mysterious *it*, and I committed to staying the course until we did. One January morning, the answer came. In truth, it didn't look like anything I had expected, but it was better than I could have ever imagined.

In the article "Memory Reconsolidation: Time to Change Your Mind," authors and researchers Bailey and Balsam note:

Ideally, we should benefit from our experiences—not remaining set in our ways, but rather being capable of flexibly adjusting our memories and representations as we encounter new information. It would be extremely inefficient to treat each experience as entirely unique and have to learn things *de novo* each time we encounter them. Being able to form memories is ultimately what allows us to learn from experience and carry information about how the world works forward in time; being able to update memories allows us to continuously adapt to changes in the world.[18]

This is where triggers play a big role. In my story, my mother's harsh prosody, or tone of voice, activated a memory or memories that still had a five-alarm negative charge attached to it. Even with all the counseling and therapy I have done, that specific tone of voice still activated me. It triggered something deep in my sub-conscious and instantly upset me. As I've come to learn, the harsh sound of her tone of voice toward my sister was something that made me feel unsafe and insecure—as a child. Those memories were stored deep in my implicit memory system.

There was a time when scientists and psychologists believed updating was impossible, but not anymore. We now understand the power of neuroplasticity—the brain's capacity to rewire.

In the simplest of terms, memory reconsolidation removes any subconscious barrier—that is, the negatively charged emotion at-tached to the memory—and allows the once-traumatic memory to finally rest safely inside the hippocampus. No longer do we live out of the fight, flight, freeze, fawn part of our brain located in the amygdala. There are four parts to the memory complex: image, thought, feeling, and bodily sensation. "Introducing the aroma of specific essential oils at the right point in the process of recall can break apart this memory complex and thereby restructure the behavioral learning connected with the memory."[19]

This was the most fascinating and astounding aspect of the Aroma Freedom Technique—its use of therapeutic-grade essential oils in memory reconsolidation. While studying for my certifica-tion as a practitioner, I learned that "the connection between our sense of smell and emotions is unlike that of the other senses because olfactory system nerves connect directly to brain struc-tures of the limbic system,"[20] particularly the amygdala and the hippocampus.

As I carefully guide clients through the twelve steps of the Aroma Freedom Technique, they breathe strategically formulated essential oils that immediately activate memory reconsolidation, remove negative energy and obstacles, and gently create new, healthy neural pathways.

The more I learned and the more I practiced, the more I thought, *Doesn't God often use the foolish things of this world to confound the wise?* (1 Cor. 1:27). Every session confounds me as I watch clients, both young and old, be surprised and confused at the same time at how something so simple can heal something so complex. I wish I could reach through this book and guide you, too, but I couldn't find a way to make that happen. Instead, go to www.janellrardon.com, and I'll be waiting for you there.

TOOL 8

Soar in Healthy Skies

EMOTION REGULATION

THE INTENTION OF TOOL 8:
I soar in the healthy skies of emotion regulation.

When a child shuts down his painful emotional side, he also loses the ability to express his joyous side. Emotions are a whole. With anger comes the ability to express delight; with sadness comes the ability to express lightheartedness. This is the breadth of emotion that allows an adult to experience intimacy with a spouse, with God, and with his children.

David Carder et al., *Secrets of Your Family Tree: Healing for Adult Children of Dysfunctional Families*

Every soul needs a good stretching now and then. At least that is what I tried to tell myself on the steps of a Kenyan home. When Ruth, the Joy Village program coordinator, gathered us all into the main foyer of the Joy Village living room, you could hear a pin drop. Six American women and four Kenyan mamas stood in a semicircle, waiting, watching, and wondering what was about to take place.

"You will be spending the night with one of the mamas and her children," Ruth said. "This way you can immerse yourself in their lives, see their ministry, and spend time with their family before going on our weekend retreat together. I think this time will benefit each of us greatly."

One of our greatest missions on this long journey to Kenya was to bless these remarkable Kenyan mamas with their first women's retreat. There they could rest and recuperate and also receive strong, restorative teaching that would strengthen their hearts, minds, and bodies for the incredibly hard job they face every single day.

Ruth's idea seemed like a good one. Our highest priority and deepest desire were to connect and cultivate long-lasting relationships. I was so in, or at least I thought I was.

One by one, she introduced us to our mama.

"Janell, you will be with Mama E," Ruth said. "She's up in her apartment—the Love House." Each separate family apartment within the Joy Village complex bears the name of one of the fruits of the Spirit. A beautiful handmade inscription hangs over the frame of the front door.

How interesting, I thought. *The main theme of my current research is the practice of love. Wow, God doesn't miss a single thing. Time to test my teaching.* I had an inkling big lessons were on the horizon of my heart. Little did I know that I was also about to physically, step-by-step, walk into an even deeper level of my own emotional healing.

When My Soul Was Stirred

Ruth's plan took me by surprise. I wasn't prepared to spend the entire afternoon and night in the apartment with the mama and her twelve children. I thought we would be visiting the families and then sleeping together as a mission team—that is, with the women I was comfortable with and in the rooms of the main building. This being my first time on the Kenya Mission Team, I just didn't know.

Did I miss the memo? I thought. I was told to bring my purse, so I had my purse. But no change of clothes, no makeup, and most importantly in my little world, no snacks. With a rare swallowing disease, I'm always hyper-concerned about what and how I will eat.

As I made my way up the stairs, something strange happened. My emotions escalated, and I began to panic. One by one, my friends left me to be with their mamas until I was all alone on those steps—me, myself, and I. I tried to move forward but just couldn't. Feeling a bit off, I braced myself against the wooden stair railing, so many thoughts going through my head.

Oh dear, seriously, what am I going to eat?

Can I drink the water?

Where will I sleep?

How will I use the bathroom?

How will I communicate?

I didn't bring anything to do with the children.
If only I had known. I could have brought coloring books,
  games, . . .

And on and on it went. The chaotic conversation inside my head continued.

The cognitive dissonance, aka stinkin' thinkin', whirling inside my head was making me a bit nauseous. It's a fact that our physical bodies respond to and escalate internal anxiety, and mine was feeling and reeling from the effects. What frustrated me the most, though, was the fact that this international adventure wasn't "my first rodeo," so all this nonsensical thinking added even more frustration at my seeming inability to calm my nerves. Why couldn't I get it together here? *C'mon, Janell, seriously? You train women to conquer their fears every day.*

My mind raced. My heart raced faster. One dominant, out-of-control mantra rang like incessant church bells: *I can't do this. I can't do this. I can't do this.* With each step, those four words got louder and louder.

They seemed to be stuck on repeat.

I seemed to be stuck on the steps.

I was emotionally frozen, stuck in the limbic center of my brain. In that moment, I was incapacitated and unable to retrieve information stored in the highly necessary rational thinking center of my brain known as the prefrontal cortex. Hence, my heart and mind disconnected at a time when I desperately needed them to connect. Trauma researcher and author of *The Body Keeps the Score*, Bessel van der Kolk, writes, "Traumatized people chronically feel unsafe inside their bodies: The past is alive in the form of gnawing interior discomfort. Their bodies are constantly bombarded by visceral warning signs, and, in an attempt to control these processes, they often become expert at ignoring their gut feelings and in numbing awareness of what is played out inside. They learn to hide from their true selves."[1]

I definitely wasn't feeling relaxed or safe in my body, even though my mind and heart knew I was safe and secure. As J. L. Moreno, the father of psychodrama, sociometry, and group psychotherapy, said, far ahead of his time, "The body remembers what the mind forgets."[2] This was the confounding and frustrating part of this entire ordeal. Thankfully, due to the healthy emotional practices I had been implementing in my daily life, I was finally able to dig deep and access them.

"Breathe, Janell, breathe," I whispered to myself. "Ground yourself. Close your eyes. Pray your brave three-word prayer, 'God, help me.'" I repeated this simple practice until I felt the stirring in my soul quiet down. It felt like hours, but probably was only minutes. And then I welcomed God into the whys, continued my deep breathing in order to gain a sense of composure, and continued up the next flight of stairs. It's all a bit of an emotional blur, but I did find my way to the top of the steps and into Mama E's House of Love. By God's grace and a whole lot of healthy self-talk and cognitive reframing, I slowly but surely moved through the fight, flight, freeze response—making my way into what I now refer to as the "flow" response.

When My Soul Was Silent

When I walked into Mama E's, she smiled, cupping her hands over her heart. "Oh, it's you!"

Unsure of whether that was a good "Oh, it's you," I was a bit reticent at first.

Two women, two completely different cultures—a Kenyan and a Mzungu (white woman), as they say in Swahili. As we looked deep into each other's eyes, something inside of me relaxed. Peace settled in, and I settled down.

She offered me some delicious chai and made me feel as though her home was my home. The atmosphere in the House of Love welcomed me and saturated every single nerve ending in my body. Slowly and with great assurance, my nervous system sent a memo from my head to my heart: "Calm down. You've got this." My fears melted in Kenyan love and before I knew it, I felt safe and loved and deeply grateful. My soul was soothed.

I went to Kenya still recovering from relational trauma, having experienced a recent tipping point of hurtful words from a close, trusted comrade.[3] Years of hurtful words and actions, both spoken and unspoken, led me to an emotional breakdown. Even though I was unconscious of my emotions still being tender to the touch, my body was on high alert. Van der Kolk shares:

> In our studies we keep seeing how difficult it is for traumatized people to feel completely relaxed and physically safe in their bodies. We measure our subjects' HRV (heart rate variability) by placing tiny monitors on their arms during shavasana, the pose at the end of most yoga classes during which practitioners lie face up, palms up, arms and legs relaxed. Instead of relaxation we picked up too much muscle activity to get a clear signal. Rather than going into a state of quiet repose, our students' muscles often continue to prepare them to fight unseen enemies.[4]

I was fighting unseen enemies of fear and panic and didn't even know it.

Life in the House of Love

Within the hour, Mama E's twelve children started coming in from school, startled a bit to see this very tall, very white, very redheaded human being standing at the door, smiling and welcoming them home. They came home in shifts, younger children first with the older ones coming in much later. Quickly, Mama E and I transitioned from complete strangers getting to know one another to mothers on a mighty mission. Dinner preparation. Homework. Chores. Showers. Evening prayers and devotions. It didn't take long before I was no longer a guest but a part of this remarkable family. Without any hesitation, little nine-year-old Salome used her persuasive skills to coerce me, a naive foreigner, to help her with her chores: fold mounds of laundry, organize the girls' closet, and polish twelve pairs of shoes. Yes, twelve pairs, twenty-four shoes. Her coy little smile hinted at how pleased she was to have this new assistant at her side.

Five-year-old Anastasia and seven-year-old Naomi needed help with writing their letters. Thankfully, the former first-grade teacher in me knew exactly how to assist. Curious Danton and Francis were mesmerized by the fluorescent indigo night-light of my very basic Timex watch. They pressed the little button so many times, the battery died in the middle of the night. And during a roaring rendition of "This Little Light of Mine,"[5] something special happened. The smiling faces of this powerful House of Love children's choir soothed my soul. It didn't matter that I came bearing no gifts. Our joyful voices, clapping hands, and tapping toes were all we needed. Laughter filled the room, and for a few minutes, none of us had a problem in the world.

Without any warning, Mama E announced lights out and we went to bed. It was nine o'clock. I couldn't remember the last time I'd gone to bed that early.

"We have to be up by 5:00 a.m.," she said. "Time to go to bed."

I climbed into the humble twin bed in Mama E's room, clothes and all. After covering myself with beautiful Kenyan blankets, I closed my eyes and silently prayed the Jesus Prayer, an ancient meditation I recently had become familiar with: *Lord Jesus Christ, Son of God, have mercy on me.*

Lights out. *Ticktock. Ticktock. Ticktock.*

I wish I could say I slept all night, but I didn't sleep a wink. I kept turning on the fast-fading indigo night-light of my Timex . . . only to see that five minutes had passed. I stumbled to the bathroom several times and tossed and turned the rest of the time.

Finally, 5:00 came. I've never been so happy to see the dawn. Mama E hopped out of bed and began the day: preparing breakfast, packing snacks (which she made the night before), administering medicine (as many of the children are in HIV/AIDS treatment protocols), and making sure all twelve of her children were dressed and ready for their long days. As soon as the younger ones left for school, she again asked if I would like a cup of chai. Only this time, she offered to teach me how to make the delicious Kenyan chai. I took out my phone and videoed the demonstration.

"What do you eat for breakfast?" she kindly asked, while stirring the chai into the boiling milk mixture. "What can I give you?"

"Maybe a piece of toast? Cup of tea?" I said, not realizing toast isn't really a Kenyan breakfast item. Within minutes, I saw one of the older boys, Michael, run out of the apartment. I thought maybe he was late for school, but then realized, when he returned, that he had gone somewhere to get a loaf of bread for my toast—my high-maintenance, very American piece of toast. Michael's radiant smile made me feel better, though, as he seemed to share the same spirit of hospitality learned in the House of Love.

A few minutes later, Mama E placed a beautiful floral plate in front of me with my toast, which looked and tasted like delicious French toast, and a few slices of fresh Kenyan papaya, which I couldn't get enough of. And, to top it all off, she boiled some water, gave me a Kenyan tea bag, and voilà, my cup of hot tea. Each bite of my breakfast filled with her beautiful heart of hospitality and love.

I opened my journal and found a card my daughter had tucked inside. It read, "Mom, how is it? I can't wait to hear about the lives and souls you've encountered so far—whom have you met? Whose face and kindness will you always remember?"

How timely, I thought.

I looked over to Mama E, sitting on the couch shelling beans for the evening meal, and knew I would remember her face and kindness forever. Words were few, but the bond between us had grown strong. I kept thinking, *I am so thankful that I pressed through my fears and stepped outside my comfort zone. I would have missed the most glorious, most precious, most beautiful experience and relationship.*

God Is a Soul Stretcher

God is in the soul-stretching business. He specializes in enlarging the souls of man so that we can taste and see the world through his eyes. The process may be painful, as tears typically accompany soul expansion. But if we can somehow open our hearts and stay with and pray through the threshold of the fight, flight, freeze, fawn phase of initial emotional alarm, we will make our way to the flow response—a possible fifth option that I feel is available to each one of us. This living-water flow response—uniquely offered through the power of the Holy Spirit—to life's hard places, spaces, and faces is what this healing journey is all about.

The Essential Nature of Emotion Regulation

What happened to me on that Kenyan step, and the process I immediately put into practice, is what psychologists call *emotion regulation*. This term has many definitions, but I love how therapist Hillary McBride describes it. She explains emotion regulation as "our learned ability to notice and experience our emotions, and then respond to them accordingly. It is like an internal thermostat, which notices and then makes changes accordingly, to help us stay emotionally within a range of feelings that is tolerable, productive, and actually appropriate."[6] It is typically considered a process—or, as we say in the Stronger Every Day community, a healthy practice—and encompasses a wide array of strategies: contemplative prayer, healthy self-talk, talking with friends, exercising, work-life balance, writing in a journal, meditation and yoga, self-care and self-compassion, hydration and nutrition, and getting proper sleep, to name a few.

On the flip side of this life-management skill is emotional dysregulation, which is "an extreme or inappropriate emotional response to a situation (e.g., temper outbursts, deliberate self-harm).[7] This typically leads to unhealthy strategies, such as numbing (alcohol and drug abuse), self-injury, isolation, physical or verbal abuse, and more recently, excessive social media use or "digital distraction syndrome."[8]

Without a doubt, my entire stuck-on-the-Kenyan-step saga serves as a prime example of my humble attempt to move from emotion dysregulation to emotion regulation. My escalating, anxious thoughts and heightened nervous system were frozen on a negative-feedback loop—my unhealthy default behavior cycle. I had seconds to reframe my mental state by implementing prayer and healthy self-talk in an effort to interrupt and short-circuit the loop.[9] "Emotions," Hillary McBride says, "are merely information."[10] They actively and consistently inform our brain—nothing more, nothing less. As we learn to interpret the vital information our emotional messages send us, life becomes healthier and far more stable.

Out of Sight, Not Necessarily Out of Mind

While writing this chapter, I realized the real reason I froze on those steps in Kenya. It's been uncomfortably tugging at me, begging me to pay attention, asking me to listen and learn, to allow God's Spirit to heal me all the way down to my good emotional bones. Because of a tight deadline, I also needed to keep moving forward, so I tried to ignore the annoying tap on my shoulder: *Notice this. Pay attention here. Dig a little deeper.* In frustration, I relented. Remember, sometimes we have to get out of our own way (see Tool 7). With a little hesitation, I surrendered to sharing this part of the story, and I pray that somehow my process of emotion regulation helps you live into your very own beautiful story.

I have traveled on international mission journeys before, but this was my first trip post–relational trauma. Even though I thought I was emotionally healed, "my body remembered what my mind forgot."[11] I had more to learn. Relational trauma expert Dr. Tian Dayton writes, "Our bodies can carry the imprint of our unprocessed, unconscious emotions and the sights, sounds, smells, and tactile sensations that surround those feelings well after the fact, in what we refer to as 'body memories,'"[12] or as some say, "somatic affect."

> We have learned that trauma is not just an event that took place sometime in the past; it is also the imprint left by that experience on mind, brain, and body. This imprint has ongoing consequences for how the human organism manages to survive in the present. Trauma results in a fundamental reorganization of the way mind and brain manage perceptions. It changes not only how we think and what we think about, but also our very capacity to think.[13]

My body was keeping score of my exhausted emotional state. As my lovely friends and mission teammates left me, one by one, I felt very alone and, unconsciously, vulnerable and afraid. Even though I didn't realize it at the time, my body, my subconscious, defaulted to anxiety. Unexpected fear set in and stirred a deep place in my soul. I felt alone and "unsafe," even though I was completely safe. Dr. Tian Dayton affirms:

> Intimate relationships provide the most basic and available paths for healing wounds to the heart. Trauma, remember, interrupts the attachment bond, causing a loss of trust and faith in life and in relationships. These wounds cannot be healed in isolation where they lay dormant—they need the re-creation of a relationship bond that stimulates them and brings them to the surface, where they can be seen and felt and healed. The painful feelings, when they come up, can feel unsurvivable, almost like an inner death, but the feelings that were repressed in order to allow us to survive can deaden our life force, keeping energy bound up and unavailable for the business of living.[14]

I didn't think I was quite ready for going it on my own, but thankfully, God was with me. He knew I was ready, or I wouldn't have been on those steps. He helped me walk up the stairs, and he had connected me to a very strong support system—all the essentials for strong recovery. When and if I needed any help, my friends would have been there in a minute. But in my heart of hearts, I knew I needed to pray through and stay with this alone—face the fear, implement my new emotional-health tools, and lean hard on God. In his wise superintendence and intentional, strategic orchestration of life events, he knew that freedom was waiting on the other side of my fear. He knew freedom was waiting for me on the other side of the world. As my body moved up the seven stairs, my heart and mind followed.

Soaring in New Emotional Skies

Shortly after my return from Kenya, I spoke to a group of young, vibrant moms. Our topic was one of my favorites: the emotional health of women. Somewhere in the middle of our lively discussion on balancing parenting and self-care and modeling healthy behavior patterns, I mentioned that I often said to my children, "Eagles fly alone; chickens run in coops. Which would you like to be?"

One mom's face lit up, and with great passion she cried out, "How do you raise an eagle? How do I teach my twelve-year-old to go against the strong pull of modern culture? Please help me. Help us!" Without taking a breath, I quickly and boldly responded, "Teach them to soar. Yes, to soar like the eagle." We only scratched the surface of a deeper conversation because time was up. Child-care workers were standing at the door.

"Please come back so we can talk more about this," they all said.

"Let's put the date on the calendar," I replied.

As I got into my car to drive home, I thought, *Where on earth did that come from? Soar?*

Later that day, it dawned on me. Soar best describes how I felt after returning from Kenya. Having risen above disabling emotions, I felt emotionally free, much like I imagine an eagle feels when soaring in the sky. No longer tethered by a dominating, negative emotion of fear, I found myself soaring in new emotional skies—seeing the world through the lens of an emotionally healthy soul.

A Tale of Two Birds: Soaring or Flapping?

The prophet Isaiah understood the tremendous power of soaring. In fact, I think we'd all agree that he recorded one of the most well-known passages of all time, Isaiah 40:31: "Those who hope in the LORD will renew their strength. They will soar on wings like eagles; they will run and not grow weary, they will walk and not be faint" (NIV). *Soar*, rooted in two powerful Latin words, *ex* meaning "out of" and *aura* meaning "breeze," takes on several significant meanings: fly or rise high in the air, maintain height in the air *without flapping wings* or using engine power, increase rapidly above the usual level.[15]

As I am ever the teacher, that invigorating conversation about soaring encouraged me to hit the books. When I discovered that soaring involved maintaining height "without flapping wings," I may or may not have gotten up and done the chicken dance. In your mind's eye, compare the visuals that soaring and flapping bring to mind. Let's put these two thoughts side by side and give them a closer look.

Soar	Flap[16]
1. Fly or rise high in the air.	1. Flutter or wave around.
2. Maintain height *without flapping wings* or using engine power.	2. Move up and down or to and fro.
3. Increase rapidly above the usual level.	3. Be agitated or panicky.
Would it be safe to say that soaring = emotion regulation?	Would it be safe to say that flapping = emotion dysregulation?

Soaring makes me think of eagles. Flapping makes me think of chickens. Both species have their specific, unique purpose and were created by God; yet we are never once told in the Scriptures to act like chickens. We are told to soar like eagles. Why? I think the answer is simple. Eagles represent independence, dignity, freedom, grandeur, and strength. Chickens, on the other hand, represent a group mentality (coops), pecking orders (competition for dominance), limited flight capacity, and clucking and flapping.

In light of these two descriptions, soaring best describes the strength emotion regulation offers our soul and flapping best describes the drain emotion dysregulation has on our soul.

We Can Soar

I want my children to soar, not flap. In no way am I trying to diminish or devalue the chicken. I love eggs—scrambled, please. But if I had to choose between the chicken and the eagle, I'm going with the eagle—especially when it comes to my children's emotional states. As a mom, my greatest desire is for my legacy, my children, to face soul-stretching experiences, circumstances, and relationships from a strong, steady, and very stable emotional foundation. This God-given capacity enables and empowers them to soar: to rise above, to see from an elevated vantage point, to possess the ability to fly—that is, to stand alone.

In his second letter to his protégé, the apostle Paul exhorts Timothy to soar. The language might be framed a little differently, but the root meaning is the same. He writes, with great passion, "For God did not give us a spirit of timidity or cowardice or fear, but [He has given us a spirit] of power and of love and of sound judgment and personal discipline [abilities that result in a calm, well-balanced mind and self-control]" (2 Tim. 1:7 AMP).

There are two significant keys to soaring:

1. "Power" in the Greek is *dynamis*, meaning "inherent power, power residing in a thing by virtue of its nature, or which a person or thing exerts and puts forth; moral power and excellence of soul; power for performing miracles."[17] Note "power residing in a thing by virtue of its nature." Sounds just like an eagle to me!

2. "Sound mind" (KJV) and "sound judgment and personal discipline" (AMP) in the Greek are *sophronismos*, meaning "an admonishing or calling to soundness of mind, to moderation and self-control,"[18] from the root *sophronizo*, meaning "restore one to his senses."[19]

Paul is telling Timothy that he can soar. I believe he's telling us the same truth.

A Tool within a Tool: Cognitive Reappraisal

Paul's words call to us; they invite us to soar above any and all habits of emotion dysregulation in our lives. They also call us into our beautiful new story.

218

One of the most helpful emotion regulation tools is cognitive reappraisal. It's what I put into practice when I froze on those steps in Kenya. This tool falls under a therapeutic method called Cognitive Behavioral Therapy (CBT) and is "one powerful way of skillfully nudging your emotions back toward baseline. . . . [It] involves recognizing the negative pattern your thoughts have fallen into, and changing that pattern to one that is more effective."[20] This tool "reframes" the negative-feedback loop—our unhealthy default—by surrounding our thoughts and minds with the truth (positive-feedback loop).

"Emotions aren't neat," writes expert Tian Dayton. "They come up at the most inopportune times."[21] When they do, we can be ready. Using the following cognitive reappraisal tool, "Seven Steps to Soaring," we can and will soar to new emotional skies of freedom:

- **S**ecure Attachment: "I am safe, seen, and secure in God's love."
- **O**pen Heart: "I am willing to stay with and pray through until my emotions come back to baseline."
- **A**ttuned[22] Emotions: "Emotions are information. I will identify and listen to what they are trying to tell me, right here in this present moment." Contributing editor for Desiring God, Jon Bloom writes, "Emotions aren't imperative; they're not your boss. They're indicatives; they're reports. . . . [They] are gauges, not guides."[23] That gives us back some control, right?
- **R**enewed Mind: "I will practice contemplative prayer and meditation in order to shape healthy thoughts and positive-feedback loops in my brain."

- **I**nformed Body: "I will pay attention and feel the physical (somatic) sensations present in my body: headache, nausea, fatigue, nervous twitch, and so on. What are they telling me? Where am I feeling them?" This keeps us "embodied" and present to ourselves.
- **N**urtured Soul: "I will practice self-compassion and self-care, giving myself room to grow. This is 'practice makes process,' not perfection."
- **G**racious Language: "I will shift from shame to grace language."

These seven steps also serve as a great review of some of our emotional tools. When we become aware and attuned to patterns of unhealthy behavior, they lose their power. When we bring them into the light of understanding, knowledge, and truth, they lose their grip. We feel a little less crazy and a whole lot better equipped. Some days will be better than others, so be sure to practice self-compassion. As my friend and now yours, Laura (see Tool 6), writes in her poem "Impossible Is Not a Word":

> impossible is not a word
> not one I often choose
> giving up is un-preferred
> for it means to fail, to lose
> and that, to me, is absurd
> when I can easily embrace
> a different view, a new word[24]

Strength Training for the Soul

Today's Heartlift: "Being able to feel safe with other people is probably the single most important aspect of mental health; safe connections are fundamental to meaningful and satisfying lives."

Bessel A. van der Kolk, *The Body Keeps the Score*[25]

Envision: A Time to Think

What if we added a fifth option to the well-known fight, flight, freeze, fawn adrenaline-charged stress response? What if we added FLOW? It wouldn't take the initial panic or adrenaline rush away, but it offers a healthy response. As heartlifters committed to strengthening our emotional and spiritual health, FLOW becomes a viable possibility. Jesus promised living water, and we can choose to believe it always comes at exactly the right time. Memorize this prayer until you embed it in your brain.[26]

God,
    *Help me **FIND** my footing.*
    *Help me **LEAN** hard on you.*
    *Help me **ONLY** speak healthy self-talk and prayer.*
    *Help me **WAIT** for the living water to flow.*
    Amen.

Mihaly Csikszentmihalyi, cofounder of positive psychology, affirms how good soul-stretching is for us. "To overcome the anxieties and depressions of contemporary life, individuals must become independent of the social environment to the degree that they no longer respond exclusively in terms of its rewards and punishments. . . . [A person] has to develop the ability to find enjoyment and purpose regardless of external circumstances."[27]

Educate: A Time to Learn

Contemplative prayer, as described by Pastor John Piper, "is a spiritual seeing. . . . This is where, when you read your Bible, you pause and you see in and through the words to the reality with your heart, and you apprehend spiritual reality. And this gives rise to a kind of praying that is spiritual and authentic and personal and warm and strong."[28]

"Surrounded by Seven" is an exercise in contemplative prayer and a cognitive reframing tool for times when you are facing something that thrusts you into emotion dysregulation. Positive thinking only goes so far; it is unsustainable. But when practiced and coupled with contemplative prayer, it can be highly effective. Emotions are God-given and inform us how to respond. Use the following chart (available at www.janellrardon.com/resources) when praying for others. I've done the first one for you.

Surrounded by Seven	Prayers and Thoughts
Isaiah 26:1: "In that day, everyone in the land of Judah will sing this song: Our city is strong! We are surrounded by the walls of God's salvation" (NLT).	*God, I may not be able to see the walls that surround my family, but I trust that they are there keeping us safe, secure, and stable.*
Psalm 5:12: "Surely, LORD, you bless the righteous; you surround them with favor as with a shield" (NIV).	
Psalm 32:7: "You are my hiding place; you will protect me from trouble and surround me with songs of deliverance" (NIV).	

Psalm 34:7: "The angel of the Lᴏʀᴅ is a guard; he surrounds and defends all who fear him" (NLT).

Psalm 125:2: "As the mountains surround Jerusalem, so the Lᴏʀᴅ surrounds his people both now and forevermore" (NIV).

Psalm 32:10: "Many are the woes of the wicked, but the Lord's unfailing love surrounds the one who trusts in him" (NIV).

Hebrews 12:1: "Therefore, since we are surrounded by such a huge crowd of witnesses to the life of faith, let us strip off every weight that slows us down, especially the sin that so easily trips us up. And let us run with endurance the race God has set before us" (NLT).

Establish: A Time to Build

Surrounded is often interpreted as encircled or encompassed and means to close something or someone in on all sides—north, south, east, and west. Close your eyes and imagine a host of heavenly wagons surrounding you—all in an effort to keep the enemies of your soul away. They

face north, south, east, and west. When God breathed into us *his* breath, that Genesis 2:7 God-sized breath, we received a spiritual endowment to manage each and every situation or circumstance we may find ourselves facing. Never forget that you are seen and surrounded by God.

TOOL 9

Save Mental Energy for the Essentials

HUMAN CONNECTION

THE INTENTION FOR TOOL 9:
I save mental energy for the essentials.

There can be occasions when we suddenly and involuntarily find ourselves loving the natural world with a startling intensity, in a burst of emotion which we may not fully understand, and the only word that seems to me to be appropriate for this feeling is joy.

Michael McCarthy, *The Moth Snowstorm: Nature and Joy*

S ometimes the grass really is greener on the other side of the fence.

While on a golf getaway with two other couples, the three "golf widows" decided to board the fancy new bullet train, Bright Line, and travel from West Palm Beach to Fort Lauderdale. Carol, our gracious host, had an agenda filled with haunts and jaunts—tasting local cuisine, experiencing the flamboyant culture, and of course shopping. Any good day on vacation includes a little retail therapy, right?

Before we left on our adventure, I had a couple hours in the hotel alone. *Ahhh!* I grabbed my journal and iPad, sporting its brand-new fancy-pants keyboard, and decided to eat breakfast by the pool. Why not collect some strength for the day ahead? Do a little devotional and connect with God? Surrounded by swaying palm trees and balmy Florida breezes, I tucked myself away at a patio table hidden in a corner of the flourishing outdoor gardens. Quiet. Secluded. Refreshing. I'd been knee-deep in writing this book for months and needed rest. From somewhere deep inside, I felt led to set an intention for the day. I'm not sure where this rose up from or why, but I am glad it did.

"God," I prayed, "help me find beauty, joy, kindness, and peace somewhere along the path of this day." It was short and simple and blew across my heart like the soft breezes floating across my breakfast respite.

"And, God," I added, "I ask this for everyone in my sphere of influence too."

I created a couple of social media memes and sent the words out to the universe.

An Orchid Tied to a Tree

Just minutes after exiting the Bright Line, we found ourselves in front of a very beautiful old home. Something caught our attention, and we slowed down to take a look.

"What is growing from that tree?" I asked, moving forward to get a closer look. "Wait, is that an orchid?"

"It definitely is an orchid. And it's tied to the tree with pantyhose," Rachel said with a laugh. "Isn't that interesting?"

The three of us stood in disbelief, fascinated by this mysterious sighting.

"Well, hello, ladies!" said a woman with a robust, joyful voice from the other side of an iron fence. "Why don't you come on in?"

"Can we?" we chimed in unison. "Thank you!"

As she opened the iron gate, I think she may have sprinkled some invisible joy dust on us. Whatever burdens I was carrying vanished the minute I crossed that threshold.

"What is this place?" I asked, feeling as if I'd just entered the magic of Burnett's *Secret Garden*. "It is stunningly beautiful."

"Hello," the nice lady said with a smile, reminding me of Nice Lady in *The Trellis and the Seed*. I couldn't help but think she had traveled through time and was now standing in front of me.

"I'm Jo Ann, master gardener and president of the Fort Lauderdale Woman's Club," she said, beaming.

"Excuse my attire," she said, whisking loose hairs from her face and brushing dirt off her jeans. "I'm getting the gardens ready for our one-hundredth anniversary celebration next week. We had to postpone it due to Hurricane Irma, which hit us hard back in the fall. We carried at least ten dump loads out of here. It was devastating. You never get used to Mother Nature's harsh treatment.

We've been rebuilding and getting it back to its beautiful self. We're getting there. Anyway, we'd sure love to have you join us."

"Oh, we're only in town for a couple of days but wish we could," we said. "You can't tell a hurricane blew through here. Your gardens are stunning."

"Well, then let me show you around," Nice Lady Jo Ann said with a big smile.

As we started down the path through the butterfly garden, I stopped for a second. I could hardly contain myself. I pulled out my phone and sent a short video to our community, telling them all about my joyous discovery.

"Can you believe this?" I said with a laugh. "Living proof of the power of setting intentions! Just a couple hours ago, I prayed and asked to find beauty and joy along today's path. Well, here we are. Let's see what else we can find."

Shared Joy Is Double Joy

The next forty-five minutes were quite magical. Borrowing the words of an old Swedish proverb, "Shared joy is a double joy; shared sorrow is half sorrow," I'd like to say that our joy was quadrupled. This surprise visit through the gardens of this hidden gem brought four women an unexpected morning of joy. Jo Ann served as our personal, and very patient, docent and historian, sharing the story of the Fort Lauderdale Woman's Club with immense pride. Founded in 1911 by a board of just eighteen women, they were first known as the Woman's Civic Improvement Association, responsible for establishing a volunteer fire department, starting the first public library, serving as an emergency shelter during hurricanes, housing the Red Cross, and even publishing newspapers.

Under the guidance of one of their earliest presidents (1912–16), schoolteacher Ivy Stranahan, known as "the First Lady of Fort Lauderdale," they spearheaded humanitarian projects that gave voice to advancing the rights of women, Native Americans, and African Americans. In 1916, Ivy and her husband, Frank, donated the land for the ground we were standing on.[1]

"Great things happened, right here," I said to myself. "Proves my point. When women gather in the indomitable spirit of unity, great movements occur."

After we toured the gardens, Jo Ann invited us inside the historical clubhouse, where we met several other members. We listened to their stories and observed their pride and passion. We felt immensely grateful for their presence. I brushed my hand across the walls, connecting to the historic heartbeat of this special space.

If the walls could talk, I thought, *what would they say?*

We didn't want to leave, but we had a full day of fun scheduled. As we moved from place to place, enjoying one another's company, I couldn't stop thinking about Jo Ann and her beautiful association of women.

Why would they selflessly give of their valuable time and blood, sweat, and tears to this association?

Why would women gather for over a century to make their city and community a better place to be?

Why didn't they quit when life got hard? They faced a multitude of hurricanes, national disasters, financial setbacks, and so much more.

Why did Jo Ann give of her masterful talents and gifts as a volunteer, receiving no remuneration for hours and hours of hard labor?

When I returned home, I found the answers to my questions in a short YouTube video, "The History of the Fort Lauderdale Woman's Club." The narrator, June Cox, shares:

> It's very important in building community that people embrace their past. That's what makes them different from any other town, any other part of the world—their history and heritage. The passion that Ivy and her women had when they first started the club, what they did, what they saw, they looked around and saw the needs and it was because they had some place to be that this all happened. They walked these floors, these same floors, these Florida pine floors, and they are still here. Just as the building was in disrepair, so our club, just like people, like families, we had our ups and downs through the years, but we are back, and it is here to stay.[2]

Wired to Connect

Much like the orchid tied to the tree trunk, we too have an innate need to be tied to others. "Social connections," writes author and columnist Emily Esfahani Smith, "are as important to our survival and flourishing as the need for food, safety, and shelter."[3] Sociobiologist E. O. Wilson says, "To be kept in solitude is to be kept in pain and put on the road to madness. A person's membership in his group—his tribe—is a large part of his identity."[4] Connecting with others is as essential as oxygen. Extroverts and introverts alike all have a need to connect, to belong, to share life. When God breathed his life into our being, he breathed into our souls this deep, beautiful desire for belonging and connection.

Master gardener Jo Ann is tied to a passionate group of women who are committed to civic and social improvement. As they beautify their little piece of the world, they beautify the worlds of both citizens and tourists.

My friend Carol said, "I've passed by this place so many times and have never looked in that direction. How have I missed it?"

"I think the orchid summoned us," I said, smiling. "Sometimes we have to stop our fierce trekking forward and allow holy interruptions and sacred sightings."

I'd like to think that my inclination to set an intention that morning also contributed to noticing and experiencing this special visit. This isn't something I always remember to do, but after this powerful connection, I'm doing it more and more. I don't want to miss anything God might have prepared for me. His agenda is always better than my agenda.

When I find life getting too busy, I often think back to that day with great fondness and joy. It reminds me of what is important in this life. What if we had missed that moment? Missed connecting with Nice Lady Jo Ann and seeing her stunning secret garden? Missed hearing stories about how they repaired that place over and over again? Missed connecting to a historical landmark that has impacted the world for a century ?

Koinonia: The Synergy of Shared Connection

The New Testament has a beautiful word for this special connection between people: koinonia, often translated as fellowship, association, community, sharing, participation, or contribution.[5] It is mentioned nineteen times in many different versions of the Greek New Testament. The first time it appears is in the book of Acts. Here, in the early Christian church, we read in detail the fellowship or koinonia of these first followers of Jesus:

The community continually committed themselves to learning what the apostles taught them, gathering for fellowship, breaking bread, and praying. Everyone felt a sense of awe because the apostles were doing many signs and wonders among them. There was an intense sense of togetherness among all who believed; they shared all material possessions in trust. They sold any possessions and goods that did not benefit the community and used the money to help everyone in need. They were unified as they worshiped at the temple day after day. In homes, they broke bread and shared meals with glad and generous hearts. The new disciples praised God, and they enjoyed the goodwill of the people of that city. Day after day the Lord added to their number everyone who was experiencing liberation. (Acts 2:42–47)

This early community embodies the power of synergy—"the interaction or cooperation of two or more organizations, substances, or other agents to produce a combined effect greater than the sum of their separate effects"[6]—and foreshadows the fruit of healthy human connection: joy. The key to healthy human connection that produces great joy is at the center of our threefold cord of emotional health and wellness: healthy sense of self, healthy behavior patterns, and healthy communication skills.

We can only wonder if Sychar, the community changed by the Samaritan woman's transformative story, became a community that exemplified and embraced koinonia.

In Kenya, I experienced up close and personal the spiritual synergy of the Acts 2:42 community. Much like Florida's Ivy Stranahan, husband and wife Richard and Judith Brown, missionaries in Africa, worked to bring healing, hope, and helping hands to the sick and impoverished of that region. Initially they opened an AIDS clinic on the grounds of Nazareth Hospital (2001), and today, Holy Family Center serves thousands of families.[7]

As members of the team, we were given the opportunity to serve the men, women, and children of this Kenyan community.

As evening fell, we gathered together in the main house to share the highs and lows of the day's work and service. We "broke bread and shared meals with glad and generous hearts" (Acts 2:46). Our leader, Jim, stoked a brilliant fire in the living room of the main house. One by one, we came in, found our place, took a seat, and rested. Surrounded by Kenyan art and cherished keepsakes of past pilgrimages, we felt we were in a sacred space.

If the walls could talk, I thought, *what would they say?*

The space invited a holy hush and time to transition from the hard work and busy schedule of the day. Candles were lit and soft worship music invigorated and refreshed. Wrapped in the spirit of koinonia, we shared rich conversation, evening devotionals, and corporate prayer. Some stories made us laugh. Others made us cry. Others were raw, real, and remain written on the walls of that sacred space. There was something special, even sacred, about the coming in and going out and then coming in again (Deut. 28:6) in the evening to a group of like-minded men and women, serving with one big, unified heart. The spiritual synergy felt in the atmosphere of that living room was the closest I have ever been to being part of the first-century church (Acts 2:42–47).

There was no comparison of whose day was better than the other, whose work was more important or vital, whose story was more interesting or powerful. Like tributaries that flow into a mighty rushing river of living water, each individual element of our work flowed into a shared ocean of meaningfulness. When you tie your heart to a work greater than yourself, there is no room for comparison; comparison is the thief of joy.[8] Not one of us wanted to let anyone or anything steal our joy.

In *The Power of the Other*, Henry Cloud gives voice to the quality of shared connection. He writes:

> Wellness depends on being in relationships, but clearly in specific ways, imparting very specific information and coding through relational interactions, energy flow, and regulation—all of which hold performance capacity in the mind, brain, and body. It's not about relationships or information; it's about both. But it's also about experiences in our relationships that cause our very mental and physical equipment to grow, develop to a higher level, and perform better than it could before. It takes relationship, but of a certain kind. The triangle of wellness must be constructed in a particular way, so that relationships, brain and mind all work together to grow our abilities past current limits.[9]

False Intimacy

Something else happened while in Kenya. During our evening prayers, we silenced digital distractions. Being disconnected from the bells and whistles of social media opened a renewed mental energy and spiritual receptivity that I found deeply satisfying. It made me realize how much time and attention I give to false connection, or what experts refer to as "false intimacy."

On the average, experts tell us that we are checking our phones 150 times a day and giving at least two hours, approximately 116 minutes—translating to five years and four months of our lifetime—to these false relationships on social media.[10] Most often, mindless scrolling leads to mindless minutes, which eventually lead to mindless hours spent swimming in the shallow end of relationships. More often than not, I feel mentally drained at the end of the day and know for a fact it is due to screen time.

Way too much screen time.

It's a subtle but very real drain on mental, emotional, and relational energy. We are not built to know everybody's business, and we must reserve mental energy for the essentials because the essentials are everything. It is important to be able to discern when enough is enough. More importantly, know "your enough"—your social media saturation point—and daily monitor "your enough" of emotional, digital dehydration because this isn't going away. In fact, I assume it will only get more advanced and, therefore, more challenging to manage. Be self-aware and highly attuned to exactly how much information your nervous system can handle well. Keep in mind that your nervous system is your body's electrical wiring, and it thrives on a steady diet of healthy emotions, high-quality connections, and contemplative practices, such as stillness, solitude, and silence.

Too much social media, information overload, and digital distraction is the complete antithesis of the living water Jesus promised not only the Samaritan woman but us as well. Do these things drain the living water right out of us?

Shared connection, on the other hand, saturates relationships. It deeply nourishes the glial cells—the highly specialized "glue" cells that support and protect our nerve cells.[11] Author Robin Weidner reminds us that "true intimacy involves knowing and being known in all your imperfections."[12] There is absolutely no way I can know and be known solely through a digital connection. As much as I love being connected to my three children, who live far from home, via various apps, nothing compares to the power of sharing a meal around our family table—imperfections and all. In fact, "research shows that loneliness and social isolation are harmful to our health: lacking social connections is as comparable a risk factor for early death as smoking 15 cigarettes a day and is worse for us than well-known risk factors such as obesity and physical inactivity. Loneliness increases the likelihood of mortality by 26%."[13] Remember, shared joy is double joy.

Kiss the Four Walls

When the time came for our Kenyan pilgrimage to end, I felt deeply torn. I desperately missed my family back home, but I now had a shared connection with an entire new community of Kenyans, especially the remarkable mamas and children of Joy Village.

On the last morning of our stay, our leader and pastor, Jim, ceremoniously gave each of the new pilgrims on the journey a beautiful Kenyan hand-beaded cross necklace. I placed it around my neck with great pride. He then said, "If you want to return, be sure to kiss the four living room walls before you leave. It's a tradition."

"Kiss the walls?" I asked. "Oh, please don't let me forget. And I'd like to hear more about this later."

The day went on and got busier and busier with the preparations to return home.

As we were loading the van for our long ride to the Nairobi airport, Jim called out, "Janell, you haven't kissed the four walls. Don't forget!"

"Oh no!" I screamed, jumping out of the van and running quickly to kiss the four walls of our Kenyan mission house. "I want to come back!"

This old African tradition hails from the beautiful memoir *The Flame Trees of Thika: Memories of an African Childhood* by Elspeth Huxley. Her parents, Robin and Tilly, left their comfortable life in England and traveled to British East Africa, known today as Kenya. As pioneering settlers, their intention was to set up a coffee plantation. This journey led them on an arduous path of deep inner growth. The way of Africa was hard, yet curious, and adventurous Elspeth found immense joy and koinonia among the Kenyan people, particularly the Masai tribe.

The day came when her family had to leave her beloved childhood home. Due to the probability of ensuing war, they couldn't stay in Kenya. Elspeth was heartbroken. As hard as life had been, her deep connection to the people brought great sadness and sorrow at leaving. She writes, "To be torn up by the roots is a sad fate for any growing thing, and I did not want to leave Thika for the unknown. Especially I did not want to leave the people and the animals of Thika, to leave Moyal and Mohammed, George and Mary, or Alec and Mrs. Nimmo, Njombo and Sammy and Andrew, or Kupanya and old Rohio, and even Kamau, and many others."[14]

Her words call back to us, don't they? As hard as life in Kenya was for her, she hated the thought of leaving there, most importantly, leaving the deep relationships she had forged with her community. She continues, "I could not believe that in a few moments the house, the garden, the farm, and everything in it would be out of sight and gone, as if on another planet; or that it was beyond my power, beyond anyone's, to freeze it, to catch it in a groove like an old gramophone record and keep repeating the same few minutes over and over, forever."[15]

Just moments before leaving, Elspeth's mother, Tilly, says something profound to her: "Kiss each of the four walls of the living room, and you will come back for sure."[16]

As silly as this might sound, this directive to Elspeth was the direct result of shared connection. Once we've experienced the power of koinonia, we'll do anything and everything to experience it again. Like Elspeth, we want "to catch it in a groove like an old gramophone record and keep repeating the same few minutes over and over, forever." Sometimes we find shared connection in the most unexpected of places with people very different from ourselves. Sometimes we have to fly halfway across the world; sometimes we simply walk next door to our neighbor's house. Both can be equally frightening. Sometimes achieving it comes easily; sometimes we have to fight for it. And sometimes we have to press through the panic of old narratives in order to write new ones. One thing is certain, when our hearts are set on finding shared connection, we will. When we do, we can't forget to kiss the four walls of the living room.

A Little Bit of Heaven on Earth

Dr. Seuss is often attributed as saying, "Don't cry because it's over, smile because it happened." The greatest gift of koinonia is sheer and unadulterated joy—big belly-laughing joy. The kind of joy that sticks to your bones and keeps you warm in the winter seasons of life. The kind of joy that walks you through cancer treatments, medical crises, and extended bouts of caregiving. The kind of joy that sinks deep into your nervous system and heals your body.

Nice Lady Jo Ann joy.

Kenyan pilgrimage joy.

Six friends feasting at a table joy.

When I discovered that joy was one of the least studied emotions, I stood up in my office, put my hand over my heart, and took a vow to do everything in my power to change that stunning and very sad fact. Researchers find joy to be a complex subject and much harder to study than happiness. "Its intricacies make it difficult to measure, so scientists tackle the tamer idea of happiness."[17]

And it seems that sadness, depression, and anxiety are of more concern, so more time and money is spent on researching these areas.

I suppose this fact shouldn't surprise us, knowing that millennials, sometimes referred to as "Generation Panic,"[18] are more anxious than any previous generation, suicide rates are on the rise, school shootings ravage young lives, racial tensions still haunt our nation, and political threats of nuclear bombs threaten world peace.

The world can be a sad, hard place to live in.

Scatter Joy

What is the answer, then, to this perplexing deprivation?

The joy of human connection, pure and simple.

Like Olaf, the beloved, jubilant snowman in Disney's blockbuster hit *Frozen*, we have to scatter more joy. We have to lock arms and say, "Enough is enough, already. Now is the time for joy." "'Joy is all about our connection to others,' explains George Vaillant [professor of psychiatry]. It's a subconscious, almost visceral feeling that appears to stem from the brain's limbic system, which is believed to control emotions, including pleasure. Unlike happiness, joy involves little cognitive awareness—you just feel good without thinking about it—but it's more enduring."[19]

Research is clear: above all else, our relationships with others matter the most. As we practice the threefold cord of emotional health and wellness, implement our heartlifting mental exercises, and live in the flow of living water beliefs, every relationship in our lives will flourish. When koinonia is unleashed in our own lives, "joy unspeakable and full of glory" (1 Pet. 1:8 KJV) will flow through our hearts, homes, and communities, filling each soul in our sphere of influence with the flow of living water. It's so close I can taste it.

Strength Training for the Soul

Today's Heartlift: "Every day, make sure that you laugh at least thirty times. . . . Consider that a small child laughs over four hundred times a day. For the average adult, the number is a paltry fifteen. . . . Sometimes, especially when you are about to achieve some kind of breakthrough, you'll get stuck, paralyzed by anxiety or uncertainty. I believe that laughter is a kind of psychological Drano designed specifically for these situations. It breaks up mental clogs, allowing your thoughts, feelings, intuitions, and actions to flow freely into areas you may never have explored."

Martha Beck, *The Joy Diet*[20]

Envision: A Time to Think

"Stop and smell the roses" is a familiar idiom with far-reaching life lessons. Naturalist and author Rachel Carson writes, "The pleasures, the values of contact with the natural world, are not reserved for scientists. They are available to anyone who will place himself under the influence of a lonely mountain top—or the sea—or the stillness of a forest; or who will stop to think about so small a thing as the mystery of a growing seed."[21] This meditative exercise is both simple and complex. It can be hard to unwind, especially after a long, arduous season of difficulty. Yet we must. Follow these prompts and see what surprising joy shows up along your path:

- Place yourself under the influence of a lonely mountaintop or the sea or . . . (The sky is your limit!)_____

- Maybe stop to consider the mystery of a growing seed or of a _____.
- Invite all five of your senses to the party. What do you see? hear? taste? smell? touch?
- Once again, notice somatic changes (bodily sensations). Where do you feel the positive emotion of joy in your body? Did you calm down? Feel happier? Have more patience? Sleep better that night?

Educate: A Time to Learn

Seeing an orchid tied to a tree invited me to ask, "Why tie an orchid to a tree?" "Many orchid lovers believe that once the plants are growing attached to trees, as Mother Nature intended, they draw warmth from the trunk and the surrounding foliage and can withstand the occasional cold front."[22] They can *withstand the occasional cold front*. Listen between the lines of this beautiful thought.

Being "tied" to others in koinonia and shared connection helps us withstand the occasional cold fronts—with the unexpected emotional frost and freezing—of life that we often pass through. Today, ask yourself, "To whom am I tied?" Use the following prompts for a short, self-guided, introspective look at how you are optimizing and enjoying healthy relationships and safe, secure social connections:

- Revisit your limiting beliefs from Tool 6. Consider how they might be hindering your ability to connect to others. As you work to reframe your limiting beliefs into living water beliefs, your social connections will grow. If you need help in this area of your life, reach out. Remember, asking for help is a sign of great strength, not weakness (2 Cor. 12:9). Gather a small group of like-minded friends and do a book study, small group, or Bible study, with this book. Let's schedule a virtual heartlifting conversation and grow together. I'd love to meet you and your friends! The book club/small group study guide and my contact information are available at www.janellrardon.com/resources.

- Consider this: We don't have to fly halfway around the world to experience the immense joy of human connection. We simply have to invite friends over. Be brave. Maybe hospitality isn't your thing, and I understand that. My introversion often gets the best of me too. But koinonia won't happen unless we open our hearts and homes and ask others to sit around our table.

- In the 1980s, anthropologist Robin Dunbar accidentally stumbled across the optimum number of friends a human being could possibly have in their social group. Based on his research, he established the following: 150 casual friends; 50 close friends; 15 confidantes; and 5 intimates, typically your best friends and often family members. "One of the things that keeps face-to-face friendships strong is the nature [and] . . . synchronicity of shared experience. . . . 'We underestimate how important touch is in the social world,' [Dunbar] said. With a light brush on the shoulder, a pat, or a squeeze of the arm or hand, we can communicate a deeper bond than through speaking alone."[23]

- Ultimately, the most powerful, most intimate, most vital relationship in life is our relationship with God through his

Son, Jesus, as expressed in and through the power of the Holy Spirit. In *Connecting*, author and counselor Larry Crabb writes, "We have all been connected by an Eternal Community of three fully connected persons. . . . In connecting with God, we gain life. In connecting with others, we nourish and experience that life as we freely share it. Rugged individualism, proud independence, and chosen isolation violate the nature of our existence as much as trying to breathe under water."[24] Continue nurturing your practices of devotion to God. As you draw close to God, he promises to draw close to you (James 4:8).

Establish: A Time to Build

Meditate on the powerful words of 1 Peter 1:8: "Though you have not seen Him [Jesus], you love Him; and though you do not even see Him now, you believe and trust in him and you greatly rejoice and delight with inexpressible and glorious joy" (AMP). In the Greek, joy or *chara* means cheerfulness, calm delight, and gladness[25] imparted by God's love to us.

To have this measure of joy is to experience the power of human flourishing. Might we say, to be heartlifted? I think so. No matter what unfolds in your story, God's design is for you to be well and to absolutely thrive. It is your birthright (Eph. 1). Somehow, this knowledge helps me get through almost anything. When I know that God has my ultimate wellness in mind, I can calmly delight in his plans and purposes. Rest might not come immediately, but I promise it will come. I leave you with the profound words of Psalm 23, interpreted so beautifully in the Voice, and may you always remember that you, my friend, have value, worth, and dignity.

The Eternal is my Shepherd, He cares for me always.
He provides me rest in rich, green fields
    beside streams of refreshing water.
He soothes my fears;
He makes me whole again,
    steering me off worn, hard paths
    to roads where truth and righteousness echo His
    name.

Even in the unending shadows of death's darkness,
    I am not overcome by fear.
   Because you are with me in those dark moments,
    near with Your protection and guidance,
    I am comforted.

You spread out a table before me,
    provisions in the midst of attack from my enemies;
You care for all my needs, anointing my head with
   soothing, fragrant oil,
    filling my cup again and again with Your grace.
Certainly Your faithful protection and loving provision
   will pursue me
    where I go, always, everywhere.
I will always be with the Eternal,
    in your house forever.

Glossary

autonomic nervous system (ANS): the portion of the nervous system innervating smooth muscle and glands, including the circulatory, digestive, respiratory, and reproductive organs. It is divided into the sympathetic nervous system (fight, flight, freeze, fawn response; directs the body's rapid involuntary response to dangerous or stressful situations; a flash flood of hormones boosts the body's alertness and heart rate, sending extra blood to the muscles) and the parasympathetic nervous system (rest and digest; conserves energy as it slows the heart rate, increases intestinal and gland activity, and relaxes sphincter muscles in the gastrointestinal tract).[1]

boundaries: a psychological demarcation that defines what is me and what is not me. It shows me where I end and someone else begins, leading me to a sense of ownership. Knowing what I am to own and take responsibility for gives ultimate freedom.[2]

cognition: all forms of knowing and awareness, such as perceiving, conceiving, remembering, reasoning, judging, imagining, and problem solving. Along with affect and conation, it is one of the three traditionally identified components of the mind.[3]

cognitive distortion: biased perspectives we take on ourselves and the world around us. They are irrational thoughts and beliefs we unknowingly reinforce over time.[4]

cognitive reframing: sometimes referred to as cognitive restructuring. It is a therapeutic process that helps a person discover, challenge, and modify or replace their negative, irrational thoughts.[5]

comparison, taken from compare (verb): estimate, measure, or note the similarity or dissimilarity between.[6] For example, Why aren't you neat like your sister? She's the stronger daughter. You are just like your father! (and note that mother wasn't fond of father).

coping style: the characteristic manner in which an individual confronts and deals with stress, anxiety-provoking situations, or emergencies.[7]

default: our go-to unhealthy cycle of thoughts and actions.

defense mechanism: a subconscious reaction pattern employed by the ego to protect itself from the anxiety that arises from psychic conflict.[8]

ego (Latin, "I"): the self, particularly the conscious sense of self.[9]

enmeshment: a condition in which two or more people, typically family members, are involved in each other's activities and personal relationships to an excessive degree, thus limiting or precluding healthy interaction and compromising individual autonomy and identity.[10]

eudaimonia (Greek): achieving the best conditions possible for being a human being in every sense—not only happiness, but also virtue, morality, and a meaningful life.[11]

family of origin: the significant caretakers and siblings that you grew up with. This can be either a biological or an adoptive family and can also be a foster home.

favoritism: giving unfair preferential treatment to one person or group at the expense of another.[12] For example, whispers pass between mother and favored child while the other stands nearby, listening. Favored child feels awkward and uncomfortable. Other child feels pain, anger, or even numbness.

Genesis 2:7 beginning: that specific moment when God breathed his breath and virtues into you, and you became a living being.

heartlift (verb): the process of vocalizing crushing pain in a healthy manner that brings closure, emotional healing, and lasting freedom.

heartlift (noun): a safe space in which families, workplaces, and churches grasp the powerful practice of the threefold cord of emotional health and wellness.

heartlifter (noun): an individual committed to the threefold cord of emotional health and wellness: healthy sense of self, healthy behavior patterns, and healthy communication skills.

heartlifting (noun): a rigorous, intentional program or "mental gym" for reframing cognitive distortions—that is, unhealthy thought patterns.

Heartlift Method, The: a threefold cognitive, emotional, and spiritual healing process that involves reflecting, reframing, and re-authoring your history of hurts into a vision of victory.

heartrift: deep wounds caused by heartbreaking words from close, trusted family members and friends.

heartshift: the moment in time when the heart awakens to truth.

history of hurts: a heart's emotional memory.

limbic system: a group of deep-brain structures, common to all mammals, which includes the hippocampus, amygdala, gyrus fornicatus, and connecting structures associated with olfaction, emotion, motivation, behavior, and various autonomic functions.

living water beliefs: God's powerful, unlimited principles and purposes for living a rich, meaningful life.

memory reconsolidation: a fairly new process of unlocking, recoding, and reorganizing the information in a memory, which allows the mind to form a healthier version of the memory.[13]

narrative: a spoken or written account of connected events; a story.[14]

secure attachment: the positive parent-child relationship, in which the child displays confidence when the parent is present, shows mild distress when the parent leaves, and quickly reestablishes contact when the parent returns.[15]

spiritual growth: creating time, energy, space, and heart to cultivate the knowledge of God in our personal lives.[16]

spirituality: the quality of being concerned with the human spirit or soul as opposed to material or physical things.[17]

spiritual resilience: not simply about recovering from adversity but about bouncing back in a way that deeper knowledge of both God and self may result. With the right guidance, during difficult times and periods of confusion, pain, and stress, we have a unique opportunity to nurture our relationship with God and enable it to grow in surprising ways.[18]

spiritual synergy: an alignment of mental, emotional, physical, and spiritual health; a true collaboration between God and man, as they work together through the rhythms of life—the good, the bad, and the ugly (Rom. 8:28).

triangulation: a situation in which two individuals in conflict each attempt to draw a third party to their side. Often expressed in nonverbal cues as well as the spoken word.[19]

trigger: a stimulus that elicits a reaction.[20]

vision of victory: the expression and fulfillment of your Genesis 2:7 God-breathed capacity and purpose.

window of tolerance: a term used to describe the zone of arousal in which a person is able to function most effectively. When people are within this zone, they are typically able to readily receive, process, and integrate information and otherwise respond to the demands of everyday life without much difficulty. This optimal window was first named as such by Dan Siegel.[21]

Resources

- Stronger Every Day online community: https://www.janell rardon.com; additional resources can be found at https:// www.janellrardon.com/resources and https://www.janell rardon.com/podcast/

- Aroma Freedom: https://www.aromafreedom.com/
- Ruth Haley Barton: https://transformingcenter.org/
- Annie Chen, LMFT: https://www.changeinsight.net/
- Beatrice Chestnut: https://beatricechestnut.com/
- Chestnut Paes Enneagram Academy: https://cpenneagram .com/
- Dr. Henry Cloud: https://www.drcloud.com/
- Ian Morgan Cron: https://ianmorgancron.com/
- Dr. Saundra Dalton-Smith: http://www.drdaltonsmith .com/
- Emotion-Focused Family Therapy: https://www.emotion focusedfamilytherapy.org/
- Dr. Antipas Harris: https://antipasharris.com/

- Diane Poole Heller: https://dianepooleheller.com/
- Dr. Caroline Leaf: https://drleaf.com/
- PACT Institute and Dr. Stan Tatkin: https://www.thepact institute.com/blog
- Positive Psychology: https://positivepsychology.com/
- Renovare: https://renovare.org/
- Gary Thomas: https://garythomas.com/
- Caroline Williams: https://www.carolinewilliamsyoga .com/

Notes

Introduction

1. Grace, "Haibun Monday #38, Kintsugi: The Art of Broken Pieces," dVerse ~Poets Pub, May 27, 2017, https://dversepoets.com/2017/05/29/haibun-monday -38-kintsugi-the-art-of-broken-pieces/.

2. "Biology of Emotion," Lumen, accessed February 19, 2020, https://courses .lumenlearning.com/boundless-psychology/chapter/biology-of-emotion/.

3. "Brain Cross-Section with Labels," iStock, accessed March 2, 2020, https:// www.istockphoto.com/vector/brain-cross-section-with-labels-gm502041209-4 3608806.

4. Tom Jacobs, "The Neurobiology of Fear," Pacific Standard, updated June 14, 2017, https://psmag.com/social-justice/the-neurobiology-of-fear-44364.

5. Pete Walker, "Codependency, Trauma and the Fawn Response," pete-walker .com, accessed March 3, 2020, http://pete-walker.com/codependencyFawnResponse .htm.

6. "Biology of Emotion."

7. Suzana Herculano-Houzel, "The Human Brain in Numbers: A Linearly Scaled-up Primate Brain," *Frontiers in Human Neuroscience* 3, no. 31 (November 9, 2009), https://www.ncbi.nlm.nih.gov/pmc/articles/PMC2776484/.

8. "Implicit memory uses past experiences to remember things without thinking about them. The performance of implicit memory is enabled by previous experiences, no matter how long ago these experiences occurred." Kim Ann Zimmermann, "Implicit Memory: Definition and Examples," LiveScience, February 13, 2014, https://www.livescience.com/43353-implicit-memory.html.

9. Benjamin Perkus, *The Aroma Freedom Technique* (Santa Barbara, CA: Aroma Freedom International, 2016).

10. John Greenleaf Whittier, "Maud Muller," Bartleby.com, accessed June 18, 2018, http://www.bartleby.com/102/76.html.

11. Julie Beck, "In a Brainy Age, the Heart Retains Its Symbolic Power," *Atlantic*, August 4, 2016, http://www.theatlantic.com/health/archive/2016/08/the -embracing-metaphors-of-the-heart-this-mortal-coil-fay-bound-alberti/494375.

12. Rollin McCraty, "The Science of HeartMath," HeartMath, October 17, 2019, https://www.heartmath.com/science/.
13. Julia August, "Hand Drawn Watercolor Illustration," iStock, accessed March 2, 2020, https://www.istockphoto.com/vector/hanging-holiday-garland-with-red-hearts-handdrawn-watercolour-graphic-illustration-gm1130350749-298918816.
14. "The Daily Examen," Ignatian Spirituality, accessed June 18, 2018, https://www.ignatianspirituality.com/ignatian-prayer/the-examen.

Tool 1 Step across the Threshold

1. "Maya Angelou," Goodreads, accessed June 18, 2018, https://www.good reads.com/quotes/23510-i-sustain-myself-with-the-love-of-family.
2. "The Human Flourishing Program," Harvard University, accessed March 3, 2020, https://hfh.fas.harvard.edu/.
3. Emily Esfahani Smith and Jennifer Aaker, "In 2017, Pursue Meaning instead of Happiness," The Cut, December 30, 2016, https://www.thecut.com/2016/12/in-2017-pursue-meaning-instead-of-happiness.html.
4. Brent Strawn, "The Bible and Happiness," Oxford Biblical Studies Online, accessed August 1, 2020, https://global.oup.com/obso/focus/focus_on_happiness/.
5. Janell M. Rardon, *Overcoming Hurtful Words: Rewrite Your Own Story* (Franklin, TN: Worthy, 2017).
6. Rebecca Solnit, *Wanderlust: A History of Walking* (New York: Penguin Books, 2001), 13.
7. "Lao Tzu Quotes," BrainyQuote, accessed July 25, 2017, https://www.brainy quote.com/quotes/quotes/l/laotzu398196.html.
8. *APA Dictionary of Psychology*, s.v. "positive psychology," accessed August 4, 2020, https://dictionary.apa.org/positive-psychology.
9. Mihaly Csikszentmihalyi, *Flow: The Psychology of Optimal Experience* (New York: Harper & Row, 2009), 3.
10. Courtney E. Ackerman, "What Is Positive Psychology & Why Is It Important?," April 16, 2020, https://positivepsychologyprogram.com/what-is-positive-psychology-definition/#flow.
11. L. B. E. Cowman, *Contemporary Classic/Streams in the Desert* (Grand Rapids: Zondervan, 2009), 52. Used by permission of Zondervan, www.zondervan.com.
12. Henry David Thoreau, "Walking," *Atlantic*, accessed July 17, 2017, https://www.theatlantic.com/magazine/archive/1862/06/walking/304674/.
13. *Cambridge Dictionary*, s.v. "saunter," June 1862, https://dictionary.cam bridge.org/us/dictionary/english/saunter.
14. Quoted in Donald S. Whitney, *Spiritual Disciplines for the Christian Life* (Colorado Springs: NavPress, 2014), 88.
15. Merriam-Webster.com, s.v. "reconnaissance," accessed June 18, 2018, https://www.merriam-webster.com/dictionary/reconnaissance.

Tool 2 Sit in God's Presence

1. Hal Shorey, "The Keys to Rewarding Relationships: Secure Attachment," *Psychology Today*, February 12, 2015, https://www.psychologytoday.com/blog

/the-freedom-change/201502/the-keys-rewarding-relationships-secure-attach
ment.

2. Shorey, "Keys to Rewarding Relationships."

3. Gary L. Thomas, *Sacred Pathways: Discover Your Soul's Path to God* (Grand Rapids: Zondervan, 2015), 23.

4. Thomas, *Sacred Pathways*, 44.

5. Thomas, *Sacred Pathways*, 47.

6. Jan Karon and Robert Gantt Steele, *The Trellis and the Seed: A Book of Encouragement for All Ages* (New York: Puffin Books, 2005), n.p.

7. Janell Rardon, *Rock-Solid Families: Transforming an Ordinary Home into a Fortress of Faith* (Chattanooga: Living Ink Books, 2007).

8. Jadwiga Leigh and Jane Laing, *Thinking about Child Protection Practice: Case Studies for Critical Reflection and Discussion* (Bristol: Policy Press, 2018), 110.

9. Marni Feuerman, "Coping with an Insecure Attachment Style," Verywell Mind, updated March 2, 2020, https://www.verywellmind.com/marriage-insecure -attachment-style-2303303.

10. Dan Siegel and Lisa Firestone, "Making Sense of Your Life," Psychalive eCourses, accessed July 8, 2017, http://ecourse.psychalive.org/making-sense-of -your-life-ecourse-dan-siegel-lisa-firestone/.

11. Christopher Bergland, "How Do Neuroplasticity and Neurogenesis Rewire Your Brain?," *Psychology Today*, February 6, 2017, https://www.psychologyto day.com/blog/the-athletes-way/201702/how-do-neuroplasticity-and-neurogene sis-rewire-your-brain.

12. Siegel and Firestone, "Making Sense of Your Life."

13. Ellie Lisitsa, "Emotional Attunement," Gottman Institute, January 16, 2014, https://www.gottman.com/blog/self-care-emotional-attunement/.

14. Lisitsa, "Emotional Attunement."

15. Lisitsa, "Emotional Attunement."

16. Quoted in Carrie Kerpen, "Stop Comparing Your Behind-the-Scenes with Everyone's Highlight Reel," *Forbes*, July 29, 2017, https://www.forbes.com/sites /carriekerpen/2017/07/29/stop-comparing-your-behind-the-scenes-with-every ones-highlight-reel/#2916dd2b3a07.

17. Timothy E. Clinton and Gary Sibcy, *Why You Do the Things You Do: The Secret to Healthy Relationships* (Nashville: Integrity, 2006), 225.

18. Oxford Dictionaries, s.v. "security," accessed July 19, 2020, https://www .lexico.com/en/definition/security.

19. Oxford Dictionaries, s.v. "insecurity," accessed July 19, 2020, https://www .lexico.com/en/definition/insecurity.

20. Wayne Jacobsen, *In My Father's Vineyard* (Nashville: Word, 1997), 63.

21. Jodi Clarke, "How to Build a Relationship Based on Interdependence," Verywell Mind, updated February 2, 2020, https://www.verywellmind.com/how -to-build-a-relationship-based-on-interdependence-4161249.

22. Clarke, "How to Build a Relationship Based on Interdependence."

23. C. E. Rusbult and P. A. Van Lange, "Interdependence, Interaction, and Relationships," *Annual Review of Psychology* 54, no. 1 (February 2003): 351–75, https://www.annualreviews.org/doi/abs/10.1146/annurev.psych.54.101601.145059.

24. "Take the Quiz," Attachment Quiz, accessed March 4, 2020, https://www.attachmentquiz.com/quiz.html.

25. Frances Hodgson Burnett, *The Secret Garden* (New York: Penguin Young Readers, 1995), 241.

26. Dan Schawbel, "Brené Brown: Why Human Connection Will Bring Us Closer Together," *Forbes*, September 12, 2017, https://www.forbes.com/sites/dan schawbel/2017/09/12/brene-brown-why-human-connection-will-bring-us-closer -together/#483068e62f06.

Tool 3 Shape Healthy Thoughts

1. James Allen, *As a Man Thinketh: The Complete Original Edition and Master of Destiny* (New York: St. Martin's Press, 2019), 13.

2. *APA Dictionary of Psychology*, s.v. "cognition," accessed June 19, 2018, https://dictionary.apa.org/cognition.

3. Janell M. Rardon, *Overcoming Hurtful Words: Rewrite Your Own Story* (Franklin, TN: Worthy, 2017), 10, 65.

4. Stephen Miller, "Waging a Crusade against Stinkin' Thinkin'," *Wall Street Journal*, November 28, 2012, https://www.wsj.com/articles/SB10001424127887 3240208045781475324000735730.

5. *Cambridge Dictionary*, s.v. "stinking thinking," accessed July 16, 2020, https://dictionary.cambridge.org/us/dictionary/english/stinking-thinking.

6. A great tool for understanding different personality types is the Enneagram. A good place to start is Beatrice Chestnut, "Empowering Change through the Enneagram," The Chestnut Group, accessed May 6, 2020, https://beatricechest nut.com/.

7. "10 Forms of Cognitive Distortions (Faulty Thinking)," Habits for Well-being, accessed June 19, 2018, https://www.habitsforwellbeing.com/10-forms-of -cognitive-distortions-faulty-thinking/.

8. Nancy Colier, "Stop 'Shoulding' Yourself to Death," *Psychology Today*, April 6, 2013, https://www.psychologytoday.com/us/blog/inviting-monkey-tea/2 01304/stop-shoulding-yourself-death-0. *Shoulding* is a term I've used for years. Take a week and observe how many times either you say, "I should," or someone else tells you, "You should." Now, there are *good shoulds*, "You should brush your teeth twice a day," but there are a whole lot more *negative*, *shaming shoulds* that reap no emotional benefit. Learning how to manage the shoulding is an asset to your emotional wellness.

9. Please learn more about your Enneagram type. As we've discussed, this emotional-health tool aids in personal growth and development in a profoundly helpful way. "Personal Development," Chestnut Paes Enneagram Academy, accessed July 16, 2020, https://cpenneagram.com/programs/personal-development/.

10. Romans 2:4 reads, "Do you take the kindness of God for granted? Do you see His patience and tolerance as signs that He is a pushover when it comes to sin? How could you not know that His kindness is guiding our hearts to turn away from distractions and habitual sin to walk a new path?"

11. Beatrice Chestnut, *The Complete Enneagram: 27 Paths to Greater Self-Knowledge* (Berkeley: She Writes Press, 2013), 2.

12. Robert Leahy, "Cognitive Assessment," American Institute for Cognitive Therapy, accessed February 21, 2020, https://www.cognitivetherapynyc.com/assessment.aspx.

13. Chestnut, *The Complete Enneagram*.

14. "The Most Accurate and In-Depth Enneagram Report Available," Ian Morgan Cron, accessed February 24, 2020, https://ianmorgancron.com/assessment. There are many different testing and assessment options. I have found the iEQ9 offered by Cron to be informative and useful, both personally and professionally.

15. Chestnut, *The Complete Enneagram*, 9.

16. Ian Morgan Cron, *The Road Back to You: An Enneagram Journey to Self-Discovery* (Downers Grove, IL: InterVarsity, 2016), 18.

Tool 4 Shift from Shaming to Gracing

1. Janell M. Rardon, *Overcoming Hurtful Words: Rewrite Your Own Story* (Franklin, TN: Worthy, 2017), 45.

2. Curt Thompson, *The Soul of Shame: Retelling the Stories We Believe about Ourselves* (Downers Grove, IL: InterVarsity, 2015), 93.

3. Thompson, *The Soul of Shame*, 44.

4. Online Etymology Dictionary, s.v. "demolish (v.)," accessed December 31, 2019, https://www.etymonline.com/word/demolish.

5. Online Etymology Dictionary, s.v. "captive (v.)," accessed December 31, 2019, https://www.etymonline.com/word/captive.

6. "Shame—Live from Seattle," *The Liturgists*, December 5, 2017, http://www.theliturgists.com/podcast/2017/12/5/shame-live-from-seattle.

7. Oxford Dictionaries, s.v. "shame," accessed June 19, 2018, https://en.oxforddictionaries.com/definition/shame.

8. Oxford Dictionaries, s.v. "humiliate," accessed June 19, 2018, https://en.oxforddictionaries.com/definition/humiliate.

9. Oxford Dictionaries, s.v. "ashamed," accessed June 19, 2018, https://en.oxforddictionaries.com/definition/ashamed.

10. Oxford Dictionaries, s.v. "disgrace," accessed June 19, 2018, https://en.oxforddictionaries.com/definition/disgrace.

11. Oxford Dictionaries, s.v. "sneaky," accessed June 19, 2018, https://en.oxforddictionaries.com/definition/sneaky.

12. Oxford Dictionaries, s.v. "underhanded," accessed June 19, 2018, https://en.oxforddictionaries.com/definition/underhanded.

13. Oxford Dictionaries, s.v. "subterfuge," accessed June 19, 2018, https://en.oxforddictionaries.com/definition/subterfuge.

14. Oxford Dictionaries, s.v. "furtive," accessed July 28, 2020, https://en.oxforddictionaries.com/definition/furtive.

15. Ian Cron, "Living Out Loud: An Interview with Jo Saxton," *Typology*, January 11, 2018, https://www.typologypodcast.com/2018/11/01/episode26/josaxton.

16. Brené Brown, *Daring Greatly: How the Courage to Be Vulnerable Transforms the Way We Live, Love, Parent, and Lead* (London: Penguin Life, 2015), 69.

17. Thompson, *The Soul of Shame*, 21.

18. Arielle Schwartz, "Embodiment in Somatic Psychology," March 25, 2017, Dr. Arielle Schwartz, https://drarielleschwartz.com/embodiment-in-somatic-psychology-dr-arielle-schwartz/#.XyBOf55KiUk. Also see the posted comments. Dr. Schwartz defines embodiment as "the practice of attending to your sensations. Awareness of your body serves as a guiding compass to help you feel more in charge of the course of your life. Somatic awareness provides a foundation for empathy, helps you make healthy decisions, and gives important feedback about your relationships with others. Embodiment in somatic psychology applies mindfulness and movement practices to awaken body awareness as a tool for healing."

19. Brené Brown, *Rising Strong* (New York: Random House, 2017), 155.

20. "Gospel of John-F.B.Meyer-2," Precept Austin, accessed July 19, 2020, https://www.preceptaustin.org/gospel_of_john-f_b_meyer-2#3.

21. "Gospel of John-F.B.Meyer-2."

22. "Head and Brain Silhouette with Heart Shape," iStock, accessed March 2, 2020, https://www.istockphoto.com/vector/head-and-brain-silhouette-with-heart-shape-gm1058086048-282778756.

23. Philip Yancey, *The Jesus I Never Knew* (Grand Rapids: Zondervan, 2002), 25.

24. John Kohlenberger III, "Jesus' Radical Treatment of Women: Destined to Cause the Falling and Rising of Many," CBE International, September 5, 2009, https://www.cbeinternational.org/resources/article/mutuality/destined-cause-falling-and-rising-many.

25. Eugene H. Peterson, *A Month of Sundays: Thirty-One Days of Wrestling with Matthew, Mark, Luke, and John* (Colorado Springs: WaterBrook, 2019), 40.

26. Peterson, *A Month of Sundays*, 52.

27. Bob Beaudine, *2 Chairs: The Secret That Changes Everything* (Franklin, TN: Worthy, 2016), 2.

28. Harriet Lerner, *The Dance of Connection: How to Talk to Someone When You're Mad, Hurt, Scared, Frustrated, Insulted, Betrayed, or Desperate* (New York: HarperCollins, 2001), xiv, emphasis original.

29. Joaquín Selva, "Why Shame and Guilt Are Functional for Mental Health," PositivePsychology.com, April 7, 2019, https://positivepsychology.com/shame-guilt/.

30. Brené Brown, *The Gifts of Imperfection: Let Go of Who You Think You're Supposed to Be and Embrace Who You Are* (Center City, MN: Hazelden, 2010), 41.

31. Thompson, *The Soul of Shame*, 93.

32. "G5485—charis—Strong's Greek Lexicon (KJV)," Blue Letter Bible, accessed June 18, 2018, https://www.blueletterbible.org/lang/lexicon/lexicon.cfm?Strongs=G5485&t=KJV.

33. Brown, *The Gifts of Imperfection*, 39.

34. "Self-Compassion," Kristin Neff, accessed March 4, 2020, https://self-compassion.org/the-three-elements-of-self-compassion-2/.

Tool 5 Speak Healing Words to Your Future

1. Hindsight taught me that trauma wounds have far-reaching effects. We carry them until we consolidate them, which is what my work in Aroma Freedom Technique accomplishes.

2. Read through this beautiful passage of promise: "You see, God takes all our crimes—our seemingly inexhaustible sins—and removes them. As far as east is from the west, He removes them from us" (Ps. 103:12).

3. Take time to pause and pray for God to reveal his new way of living your life. Allow these words to wash over you: "Therefore, if anyone is united with the Anointed One, that person is a new creation. The old life is gone—and see—a new life has begun!" (2 Cor. 5:17).

4. David Whyte, "Regret," in *Consolations: The Solace, Nourishment and Underlying Meaning of Everyday Words* (Langley, WA: Many Rivers Press, 2014), accessed June 19, 2018, http://www.davidwhyte.com/essays/.

5. Marcus Borg, *Meeting Jesus Again for the First Time: The Historical Jesus and the Heart of Contemporary Faith* (Waterville, ME: Thorndike, 2006), 88.

6. Gregg Levoy, *Callings: Finding and Following an Authentic Life* (London: HarperCollins, 1998), 4.

7. Janell M. Rardon, *Overcoming Hurtful Words: Rewrite Your Own Story* (Franklin, TN: Worthy, 2017), 10.

8. "Woman of Samaria," Bible Gateway, accessed June 19, 2018, https://www.biblegateway.com/resources/all-women-bible/Woman-Samaria.

9. "Stress Management," Mayo Clinic, May 9, 2017, https://www.mayoclinic.org/healthy-lifestyle/stress-management/in-depth/assertive/art-20044644?pg=2.

10. Begin by searching for qualified counselors or certified coaches. Here are a couple of good places to start: https://www.psychologytoday.com/us and https://www.aacc.net/.

11. Peacemaker Ministries, accessed June 19, 2018, https://pm.training/.

12. Stephen Henn, "The Power of a Human Voice," Medium, December 12, 2016, https://medium.com/@HennsEggs/the-power-of-a-human-voice-48177b786fa3.

13. "Stress Management."

14. "How to Be Assertive: Asking for What You Want Firmly and Fairly," MindTools.com, accessed June 19, 2018 (subscription required), https://www.mindtools.com/pages/article/Assertiveness.htm.

15. "How to Be Assertive."

16. Rardon, *Overcoming Hurtful Words*, 93–109. To rest is to recover strength.

17. Robert J. Wicks, *Availability: The Challenge and the Gift of Being Present* (Notre Dame, IN: Sorin Books, 2015), 23.

Tool 6 Soak in Living Water

1. "Arthrogryposis Multiplex Congenita," AANEM, accessed February 23, 2020, https://www.aanem.org/Patients/Muscle-and-Nerve-Disorders/Arthrogryposis-Multiplex-Congenita.

2. *Merriam-Webster*, s.v. "disability," accessed June 19, 2018, https://www.merriam-webster.com/dictionary/disability.

3. Oxford Dictionaries, s.v. "inspire," accessed July 20, 2020, https://en.oxford dictionaries.com/definition/inspire.

4. Richard Winter, *The Roots of Sorrow: Reflections on Depression and Hope* (Eugene, OR: Wipf & Stock, 2000), 150.

5. Oxford Dictionaries, s.v. "limit," accessed July 20, 2020, https://en.oxford dictionaries.com/definition/limit.

6. The Free Dictionary, s.v. "limitation," accessed June 19, 2018, https://www .thefreedictionary.com/limitation.

7. The Free Dictionary, s.v. "unlimited," accessed June 19, 2018, https://www .thefreedictionary.com/unlimited.

8. "Meet Dr. Henry Cloud," Dr. Henry Cloud, accessed February 24, 2020, https://www.drcloud.com/.

9. Robert Christian, "Fr. James Martin on 'Disordered Attachments,'" Millennial, December 5, 2013, https://millennialjournal.com/2013/12/05/fr-james -martin-on-disordered-attachments/.

10. Brené Brown, *Braving the Wilderness: The Quest for True Belonging and the Courage to Stand Alone* (Waterville, ME: Thorndike, 2018), 69.

11. Donna Hicks, "What Is the Real Meaning of Dignity?," *Psychology Today*, April 10, 2013, https://www.psychologytoday.com/us/blog/dignity/201304/what -is-the-real-meaning-dignity-0.

12. Steve Sisgold, "Limited Beliefs," *Psychology Today*, June 4, 2013, https:// www.psychologytoday.com/us/blog/life-in-body/201306/limited-beliefs.

13. Sisgold, "Limited Beliefs."

14. Sarah Peterson, "63 Toxic Beliefs That Are Poisoning Your Potential as an Entrepreneur," Unsettle, January 19, 2015, http://unsettle.org/limiting-beliefs/.

15. "G2198—zaō—Strong's Greek Lexicon (KJV)," Blue Letter Bible, accessed June 19, 2018, https://www.blueletterbible.org//lang/Lexicon/Lexicon.cfm?Strongs =G2198&t=KJV.

16. "The KJV New Testament Greek Lexicon," s.v. "Zao," Bible Study Tools, accessed February 24, 2020, https://www.biblestudytools.com/lexicons/greek/kjv /zao.html.

17. Richard Rohr, *Everything Belongs: The Gift of Contemplative Prayer* (New York: Crossroad, 2003), 101, brackets and emphasis original.

18. Be sure to subscribe to my podcast: https://www.janellrardon.com/podcast/.

19. Rohr, *Everything Belongs*, 22, 24.

Tool 7 Send New, Positive Messages to Your Brain

1. "Window of Tolerance," Good Therapy, last updated August 8, 2016, https:// www.goodtherapy.org/blog/psychpedia/window-of-tolerance.

2. "Guide for Families Part I: The Addiction Problem and Approaching It," American Addiction Centers, last updated February 3, 2020, https://american addictioncenters.org/guide-for-families-i.

3. Janell Rardon, "S3E12 The Anatomy of Repression," SoundCloud, accessed July 21, 2020, https://soundcloud.com/janell-rardon/s3e12-the-anatomy-of.

4. University of Alberta Sexual Assault Centre, "What Is a Trigger?," Psych Central, last updated October 8, 2018, https://psychcentral.com/lib/what-is-a-trigger/.

5. University of Alberta, "What Is a Trigger?"

6. Amy Morin, "Healthy Coping Skills for Uncomfortable Emotions," Verywell Mind, January 4, 2020, https://www.verywellmind.com/forty-healthy-coping-skills-4586742. There are two types of coping skills: problem-focused (finding practical, tactical solutions, such as time management, a new job, and so on) and emotion-focused (learning how to manage emotions and feelings in a healthy way).

7. Peter O'Hanrahan, "Defense Systems," The Enneagram at Work, accessed August 3, 2020, https://theenneagramatwork.com/defense-systems.

8. Saul McLeod, "Defense Mechanisms," Simply Psychology, April 10, 2019, https://www.simplypsychology.org/defense-mechanisms.html.

9. Janell M. Rardon, *Overcoming Hurtful Words: Rewrite Your Own Story* (Franklin, TN: Worthy, 2017).

10. Patty Mulder, "Albert Mehrabian's Communication Model: 7–38–55," ToolsHero, October 14, 2013, https://www.toolshero.com/communication-skills/communication-model-mehrabian/.

11. Jeffrey A. Kottler, "What REALLY Leads to Change in People's Lives?," *Psychology Today*, July 24, 2013, https://www.psychologytoday.com/us/blog/change/201307/what-really-leads-change-in-people-s-lives.

12. The Free Dictionary, s.v. "emotional literacy," accessed June 19, 2018, https://www.thefreedictionary.com/emotional+literacy.

13. Hokuma Karimova, "The Emotion Wheel: What It Is and How to Use It," PositivePsychology.com, July 4, 2019, https://positivepsychology.com/emotion-wheel/.

14. Alan Watkins, "How Controlling Your Emotional Responses Can Improve Your Performance at Work," Training, October 29, 2014, https://trainingmag.com/how-controlling-your-emotional-responses-can-improve-your-performance-work/.

15. Karimova, "The Emotion Wheel."

16. Artellia, "Plutchiks Wheel of Emotions, Psychology Diagram, Coaching Tool," accessed June 19, 2020, https://www.shutterstock.com/image-vector/plutchiks-wheel-emotions-psychology-diagram-coaching-335549708.

17. Benjamin Perkus, "The Aroma Freedom Technique," Aroma Freedom, accessed July 21, 2020, https://www.aromafreedom.com/.

18. Matthew R. Bailey and Peter D. Balsam, "Memory Reconsolidation: Time to Change Your Mind," *Current Biology* 23, no. 6 (March 18, 2013): R243–45, https://www.ncbi.nlm.nih.gov/pmc/articles/PMC4864982/.

19. "Aroma Therapy Technique," A Ministry of Light and Life Energy, accessed December 30, 2019, http://light-life-energy.com/aroma-freedom-technique-aft.

20. Regina Bailey, "The Olfactory System and Your Sense of Smell," ThoughtCo, December 3, 2019, https://www.thoughtco.com/olfactory-system-4066176.

Tool 8 Soar in Healthy Skies

1. Bessel A. van der Kolk, *The Body Keeps the Score: Brain, Mind, and Body in the Healing of Trauma* (New York: Penguin, 2015), 98–99.

2. Tian Dayton, *Relationship Trauma Repair (RTR): An Experiential, Multi-Sensory Process for Healing PTSD: Therapist's Guide* (Deerfield Beach, FL: Unrivaled Books, 2011), 17.

3. Janell M. Rardon, *Overcoming Hurtful Words: Rewrite Your Own Story* (Franklin, TN: Worthy, 2017).

4. Van der Kolk, *The Body Keeps the Score*, 273.

5. Wikipedia, s.v. "This Little Light of Mine," last edited May 13, 2020, https://en.wikipedia.org/wiki/This_Little_Light_of_Mine.

6. Hillary L. McBride, *Mothers, Daughters, and Body Image: Learning to Love Ourselves as We Are* (New York: Post Hill Press, 2017), 177.

7. *APA Dictionary of Psychology*, s.v. "dysregulation," accessed June 19, 2018, https://dictionary.apa.org/dysregulation.

8. "Digital Distraction," Digital Responsibility, accessed June 19, 2018, http://www.digitalresponsibility.org/digital-distraction/.

9. "Improve Your Perspective Using Cognitive Reappraisal," Cognitive Behavioral Therapy, May 4, 2014, http://cogbtherapy.com/cbt-blog/2014/5/4/hhy104os08dekc537dlw7nvopzyi44.

10. "Shame—Live from Seattle," *The Liturgists*, December 5, 2017, http://www.theliturgists.com/podcast/2017/12/5/shame-live-from-seattle.

11. Victor L. Schermer, "Psychodrama in Perspective: An Interview with Jonathan Moreno on His Father, Jacob Moreno, and the Lasting Impact of His Ideas," *Group Analysis* 48, no. 2 (May 26, 2015): 187–201, http://journals.sagepub.com/doi/abs/10.1177/0533316415580539.

12. Tian Dayton, "What Do We Mean by Relationship Trauma?," Central Valley Recovery Services, March 3, 2017, http://cvrshome.com/hot-topics.php?Hot-Topics-9.

13. Van der Kolk, *The Body Keeps the Score*, 21.

14. Tian Dayton, *Heartwounds: The Impact of Unresolved Trauma and Grief on Relationships* (Deerfield Beach, FL: Health Communications, 1997), 137.

15. Oxford Dictionaries, s.v. "soar," accessed June 18, 2018, https://en.oxforddictionaries.com/definition/soar, emphasis added.

16. Oxford Dictionaries, s.v. "flap," accessed June 19, 2018, https://en.oxforddictionaries.com/definition/flap.

17. "G1411—dynamis—Strong's Greek Lexicon (KJV)," Blue Letter Bible, accessed June 19, 2018, https://www.blueletterbible.org//lang/Lexicon/Lexicon.cfm?Strongs=G1411&t=KJV.

18. "G4995—sōphronismos—Strong's Greek Lexicon (KJV)," Blue Letter Bible, accessed July 21, 2020, https://www.blueletterbible.org//lang/Lexicon/Lexicon.cfm?Strongs=G4995&t=KJV.

19. "G4994—sōphronizō—Strong's Greek Lexicon (KJV)," Blue Letter Bible, accessed July 21, 2020, https://www.blueletterbible.org//lang/lexicon/lexicon.cfm?Strongs=G4994&t=KJV.

20. "Improve Your Perspective Using Cognitive Reappraisal."

21. Dayton, "What Do We Mean by Relationship Trauma?"

22. APA *Dictionary of Psychology*, s.v. "attunement," accessed June 19, 2018, https://dictionary.apa.org/attunement.

23. Jon Bloom, "Your Emotions Are a Gauge, Not a Guide," Desiring God, August 3, 2012, https://www.desiringgod.org/articles/your-emotions-are-a-gauge -not-a-guide.

24. Laura C. Robb, *Beyond: Limits, Longings, Love, Loss* (Pennsauken, NJ: BookBaby, 2019), 22, used with permission.

25. Van der Kolk, *The Body Keeps the Score*, 81.

26. "In Praise of Memorization: 10 Proven Brain Benefits," BestCollegesOn-line, accessed August 22, 2019, https://www.bestcollegesonline.com/blog/in-praise -of-memorization-10-proven-brain-benefits/.

27. Mihaly Csikszentmihalyi, *Flow: The Psychology of Optimal Experience* (New York: Harper & Row, 2009), 16.

28. John Piper, "What Do You Think about Contemplative Prayer?," Desiring God, May 22, 2010, https://www.desiringgod.org/interviews/what-do-you-think -about-contemplative-prayer.

Tool 9 Save Mental Energy for the Essentials

1. "Our History," Fort Lauderdale Woman's Club, accessed June 19, 2018, http://fortlauderdalewomansclub.com/our-history.

2. "History of the Fort Lauderdale Woman's Club," YouTube, February 13, 2014, https://www.youtube.com/watch?v=b6vnLz2fDWI.

3. Emily Esfahani Smith, "Social Connection Makes a Better Brain," *Atlantic*, October 29, 2013, https://www.theatlantic.com/health/archive/2013/10/social-con nection-makes-a-better-brain/280934/.

4. Maria Popova, "E.O. Wilson on How We Give Meaning to Life," Brain Pickings, September 18, 2015, https://www.brainpickings.org/2014/11/04/e-o -wilson-the-meaning-of-human-existence/.

5. "Koinonia: What the Bible Means by 'Fellowship,'" Bible Study Tools, March 5, 2014, https://www.biblestudytools.com/bible-study/topical-studies /koinonia-what-the-bible-means-by-fellowship.html.

6. Oxford Dictionaries, s.v. "synergy," accessed June 19, 2018, https://en.oxford dictionaries.com/definition/synergy.

7. Tree of Lives, accessed June 19, 2018, http://www.treeoflives.org/.

8. Amy Summerville, "Is Comparison Really the Thief of Joy?," *Psychology Today*, March 21, 2019, https://www.psychologytoday.com/us/blog/multiple -choice/201903/is-comparison-really-the-thief-joy.

9. Henry Cloud, *The Power of the Other* (New York: HarperCollins, 2016), 16.

10. Evan Asano, "How Much Time Do People Spend on Social Media? [Info-graphic]," Social Media Today, January 4, 2017, https://www.socialmediatoday .com/marketing/how-much-time-do-people-spend-social-media-infographic.

11. Kim Ann Zimmermann, "Nervous System: Facts, Function & Diseases," Live Science, February 14, 2018, https://www.livescience.com/22665-nervous -system.html.

12. Robin Weidner, "The Enticing Fruit of False Intimacy," Focus on the Family, January 1, 2008, https://www.focusonthefamily.com/marriage/sex-and-intimacy /building-a-pure-marriage/the-enticing-fruit-of-false-intimacy.

13. "Loneliness Research," Campaign to End Loneliness, accessed June 4, 2020, https://www.campaigntoendloneliness.org/loneliness-research/.

14. Elspeth Huxley, *The Flame Trees of Thika: Memories of an African Childhood* (London: Vintage Classic, 2014), 264.

15. Huxley, *The Flame Trees of Thika*, 274.

16. Huxley, *The Flame Trees of Thika*, 268.

17. Jessica Cerretani, "The Contagion of Happiness," Harvard Medicine, accessed June 19, 2018, https://hms.harvard.edu/magazine/science-emotion/con tagion-happiness.

18. Niamh Delmar, "Generation Panic: Why Is There So Much Anxiety among Millennials?," *Irish Times*, June 11, 2018, https://www.irishtimes.com/life-and -style/health-family/generation-panic-why-is-there-so-much-anxiety-among -millennials-1.3521341.

19. Cerretani, "The Contagion of Happiness."

20. Martha Beck, *The Joy Diet: 10 Daily Practices for a Happier Life* (New York: Crown, 2003), 152–53.

21. Maria Popova, "Rachel Carson on Science and Our Spiritual Bond with Nature," Brain Pickings, September 20, 2017, https://www.brainpickings.org/20 17/09/20/rachel-carson-lost-woods-the-real-world-around-us/.

22. Christine Winter Juneau, "Display Your Orchids as Mother Nature Intended . . . with Pantyhose," *South Florida Sun-Sentinel*, February 13, 2009, https://www.sun-sentinel.com/news/fl-xpm-2009-02-13-0902110340-story.html.

23. Maria Konnikova, "The Limits of Friendship," *New Yorker*, October 7, 2014, https://www.newyorker.com/science/maria-konnikova/social-media-affect -math-dunbar-number-friendships.

24. Larry Crabb, *Connecting: Healing Ourselves and Our Relationships* (Nashville: W Publishing Group, 2006), 53.

25. "G5479—chara—Strong's Greek Lexicon (KJV)," Blue Letter Bible, accessed June 7, 2018, https://www.blueletterbible.org//lang/Lexicon/Lexicon.cfm ?Strongs=G5479&t=KJV.

Glossary

1. *APA Dictionary of Psychology*, s.v. "autonomic nervous system (ANS)," accessed March 3, 2020, https://dictionary.apa.org/autonomic-nervous-system.

2. "What Do You Mean 'Boundaries'? by Dr. Henry Cloud and Dr. John Townsend," Cloud-Townsend Resources, March 9, 2016, https://www.cloudtownsend .com/what-do-you-mean-boundaries-by-dr-henry-cloud-and-dr-john-townsend/.

3. *APA Dictionary of Psychology*, s.v. "cognition," accessed June 19, 2018, https://dictionary.apa.org/cognition.

4. Courtney E. Ackerman, "CBT's Cognitive Restructuring (CR) for Tackling Cognitive Distortions," Positive Psychology, April 7, 2019, https://positivepsychol ogy.com/cbt-cognitive-restructuring-cognitive-distortions/.

5. Ackerman, "CBT's Cognitive Restructuring."

6. Oxford Dictionaries, s.v. "compare," accessed June 19, 2018, https://en.ox forddictionaries.com/definition/compare.

7. *APA Dictionary of Psychology*, s.v. "coping style," accessed June 18, 2018, https://dictionary.apa.org/coping-style.

8. *APA Dictionary of Psychology*, s.v. "defense mechanism," accessed June 18, 2018, https://dictionary.apa.org/defense-mechanism.

9. *APA Dictionary of Psychology*, s.v. "ego," accessed June 18, 2018, https:// dictionary.apa.org/ego.

10. *APA Dictionary of Psychology*, s.v. "enmeshment," accessed December 12, 2019, https://dictionary.apa.org/enmeshment.

11. "Eudaimonia," Philosophy Terms, accessed July 22, 2020, https://philos ophyterms.com/eudaimonia/.

12. Oxford Dictionaries, s.v. "favoritism," accessed October 23, 2018, https:// en.oxforddictionaries.com/definition/favoritism.

13. "Memory Reconsolidation: Definition, Theory, & Example," Study.com, accessed April 1, 2020, https://study.com/academy/lesson/memory-reconsolidation -definition-theory-example.html.

14. Oxford Dictionaries, s.v. "narrative," accessed October 23, 2018, https:// en.oxforddictionaries.com/definition/narrative.

15. *APA Dictionary of Psychology*, s.v. "secure attachment," accessed July 22, 2020, https://dictionary.apa.org/secure-attachment.

16. "A. W. Tozer on Spiritual Growth," Hope Church, accessed June 4, 2020, http://thisishope.org/a-w-tozer-on-spiritual-growth/.

17. Oxford Dictionaries, s.v. "spirituality," accessed December 31, 2019, https://en.oxforddictionaries.com/definition/spiritualityhttps://www.lexico.com /en/definition/spirituality.

18. Frederic and Mary Ann Brussart, review of *Spiritual Resilience*, by Robert J. Wicks, Spirituality and Practice, accessed December 31, 2019, https://www .spiritualityandpractice.com/book-reviews/view/27823/spiritual-resilience.

19. *APA Dictionary of Psychology*, s.v. "triangulation," accessed December 31, 2019, https://dictionary.apa.org/triangulation.

20. *APA Dictionary of Psychology*, s.v. "trigger," accessed June 18, 2018, https://dictionary.apa.org/trigger.

21. "Window of Tolerance," Good Therapy, last updated August 8, 2016, https://www.goodtherapy.org/blog/psychpedia/window-of-tolerance.

Janell Rardon, MA, is a Board-Certified Life Coach (AACC), an adjunct professor, and an award-winning author who loves nothing more than helping family systems become emotionally healthy, happy, and whole. In her private practice, The Heartlift Practice, she specializes in trauma-informed, attachment-based, faith-infused modalities. She and her husband of more than thirty-five years have three grown children and live in Virginia.

CONNECT
WITH
Janell

Visit **janellrardon.com** to learn about Janell's
speaking, therapy, blog, and podcast.

---

[f] JanellRardonAuthor　　[tw] janellrardon

[ig] janellrardon　　　　　[yt] Janell Rardon, MA

More resources available on Janell's blog

Head to **janellrardon.com/blog** for additional writings, resources, pdfs, short videos, and links to articles and sites. You'll be one step closer to becoming stronger than ever!